STRANGE INTERLUDE

EUGENE O'NEILL

A Play

STRANGE INTERLUDE

NEW YORK
BONI & LIVERIGHT
1928

CHARACTERS

Charles Marsden

Professor Henry Leeds

Nina Leeds, his daughter

Edmund Darrell

Sam Evans

Mrs. Amos Evans, Sam's mother

Gordon Evans

Madeline Arnold

SCENES

First Part

ACT ONE

Library, the Leeds' home in a small university town of New England—an afternoon in late summer.

ACT TWO

The same. Fall of the following year. Night.

ACT THREE

Dining room of the Evans' homestead in northern New York state—late spring of the next year. Morning.

ACT FOUR

The same as Acts One and Two. Fall of the same year. Evening.

ACT FIVE

Sitting room of small house Evans has rented in a seashore suburb near New York. The following April. Morning.

Second Part

ACT SIX

The same. A little over a year later. Evening.

ACT SEVEN

Sitting room of the Evans' apartment on Park Avenue. Nearly eleven years later. Early afternoon.

ACT EIGHT

Section of afterdeck of the Evans' cruiser anchored near the finish line at Poughkeepsie. Ten years later. After-noon.

ACT NINE

A terrace on the Evans' estate on Long Island. Several months later. Late afternoon.

FIRST PART
ACT ONE

STRANGE INTERLUDE

ACT ONE

SCENE: *The library of* PROFESSOR LEEDS' *home in a small
university town in New England. This room is at the
front part of his house with windows opening on the
strip of lawn between the house and the quiet residential
street. It is a small room with a low ceiling. The
furniture has been selected with a love for old New
England pieces. The walls are lined almost to the
ceiling with glassed-in bookshelves. These are packed
with books, principally editions, many of them old and
rare, of the ancient classics in the original Greek and
Latin, of the later classics in French and German and
Italian, of all the English authors who wrote while s was
still like an f and a few since then, the most modern
probably being Thackeray. The atmosphere of the
room is that of a cosy, cultured retreat, sedulously
built as a sanctuary where, secure with the culture of
the past at his back, a fugitive from reality can view the
present safely from a distance, as a superior with condescending disdain, pity, and even amusement.*

*There is a fair-sized table, a heavy armchair, a rocker,
and an old bench made comfortable with cushions. The
table, with the Professor's armchair at its left, is arranged toward the left of the room, the rocker is at
center, the bench at right.*

11

There is one entrance, a door in the right wall, rear.

It is late afternoon of a day in August.   Sunshine, cooled and dimmed in the shade of trees, fills the room with a soothing light.

The sound of a MAID'S VOICE—*a middle-aged woman— explaining familiarly but respectfully from the right, and* MARSDEN *enters.   He is a tall thin man of thirty-five, meticulously well-dressed in tweeds of distinctly English tailoring, his appearance that of an Anglicized New England gentleman.   His face is too long for its width, his nose is high and narrow, his forehead broad, his mild blue eyes those of a dreamy self-analyst, his thin lips ironical and a bit sad.   There is an indefinable feminine quality about him, but it is nothing apparent in either appearance or act.   His manner is cool and poised.   He speaks with a careful ease as one who listens to his own conversation.   He has long fragile hands, and the stoop to his shoulders of a man weak muscularly, who has never liked athletics and has always been regarded as of delicate constitution.   The main point about his personality is a quiet charm, a quality of appealing, inquisitive friendliness, always willing to listen, eager to sympathize, to like and to be liked.*

MARSDEN

[*Standing just inside the door, his tall, stooped figure leaning back against the books—nodding back at the* MAID *and smiling kindly*]

I'll wait in here, Mary.

[*His eyes follow her for a second, then return to gaze around the room slowly with an appreciative relish for*

the familiar significance of the books.   He smiles affec-
tionately and his amused voice recites the words with a
rhetorical resonance]

Sanctum Sanctorum!

[*His voice takes on a monotonous musing quality, his eyes*
stare idly at his drifting thoughts]

How perfectly the Professor's unique haven! . . .

[*He smiles*]

Primly   classical . . . when   New   Englander   meets
Greek! . . .

[*Looking at the books now*]

He hasn't added one book in years . . . how old was
I when I first came here? . . . six . . . with my
father . . . father . . . how dim his face has grown!
. . . he wanted to speak to me just before he died . . .
the hospital . . . smell of iodoform in the cool halls . . .
hot summer . . . I bent down . . . his voice had withdrawn so far away . . . I couldn't understand him . . .
what son can ever understand? . . . always too near, too
soon, too distant or too late! . . .

[*His face has become sad with a memory of the be-*
wildered suffering of the adolescent boy he had been at
the time of his father's death.   Then he shakes his head,
flinging off his thoughts, and makes himself walk about
the room]

What memories on such a smiling afternoon! . . . this
pleasant old town after three months . . . I won't go to
Europe again . . . couldn't write a line there . . . how
answer the fierce question of all those dead and maimed?
. . . too big a job for me! . . .

[*He sighs—then self-mockingly*]

But back here . . . it is the interlude that gently questions . . . in this town dozing . . . decorous bodies moving with circumspection through the afternoons . . . their
habits affectionately chronicled . . . an excuse for weav-

ing amusing words . . . my novels . . . not of cosmic
importance, hardly . . .

[*Then self-reassuringly*]

but there is a public to cherish them, evidently . . . and
I can write! . . . more than one can say of these modern
sex-yahoos! . . . I must start work tomorrow . . . I'd
like to use the Professor in a novel sometime . . . and
his wife . . . seems impossible she's been dead six
years . . . so aggressively his wife! . . . poor Professor!
now it's Nina who bosses him . . . but that's different . . . she has bossed me, too, ever since she was
a baby . . . she's a woman now . . . known love and
death . . . Gordon brought down in flames . . . two
days before the armistice . . . what fiendish irony! . . .
his wonderful athlete's body . . . her lover . . . charred
bones in a cage of twisted steel . . . no wonder she broke
down . . . Mother said she's become quite queer lately
. . . Mother seemed jealous of my concern . . . why
have I never fallen in love with Nina? . . . could I? . . .
that way . . . used to dance her on my knee . . . sit her
on my lap . . . even now she'd never think anything
about it . . . but sometimes the scent of her hair and
skin . . . like a dreamy drug . . . dreamy! . . . there's
the rub! . . . all dreams with me! . . . my sex life
among the phantoms! . . .

[*He grins torturedly*]

Why? . . . oh, this digging in gets nowhere . . . to the
devil with sex! . . . our impotent pose of today to beat
the loud drum on fornication! . . . boasters . . .
eunuchs parading with the phallus! . . . giving themselves away . . . whom do they fool? . . . not even
themselves! . . .

[*His face suddenly full of an intense pain and disgust*]

Ugh! . . . always that memory! . . . why can't I ever
forget? . . . as sickeningly clear as if it were yes-

terday . . . prep school . . . Easter vacation . . . Fatty
Boggs and Jack Frazer . . . that house of cheap vice
. . . one dollar! . . . why did I go? . . . Jack, the dead
game sport . . . how I admired him! . . . afraid of his
taunts . . . he pointed to the Italian girl . . . "Take
her!" . . . daring me . . . I went . . . miserably frightened . . . what a pig she was! . . . pretty vicious face
under caked powder and rouge . . . surly and contemptuous . . . lumpy body . . . short legs and thick ankles . . .
slums of Naples . . . "What you gawkin' about? Git a
move on, kid" . . . kid! . . . I *was* only a kid! . . . six-
teen . . . test of manhood . . . ashamed to face Jack
again unless . . . fool! . . . I might have lied to him!
. . . but I honestly thought that wench would feel humili-
ated if I . . . oh, stupid kid! . . . back at the hotel I
waited till they were asleep . . . then sobbed . . . thinking of Mother . . . feeling I had defiled her . . . and
myself . . . forever! . . .

[*Mocking bitterly*]

"Nothing half so sweet in life as love's young dream,"
what? . . .

[*He gets to his feet impatiently*]

Why does my mind always have to dwell on that? . . .
too silly . . . no importance really . . . an incident such
as any boy of my age . . .

[*He hears someone coming quickly from the right and
turns expectantly.* PROFESSOR LEEDS *enters, a pleased
relieved expression fighting the flurried worry on his face.
He is a small, slender man of fifty-five, his hair gray, the
top of his head bald. His face, prepossessing in spite
of its too-small, over-refined features, is that of a retir-
ing, studious nature. He has intelligent eyes and a smile
that can be ironical. Temperamentally timid, his defense
is an assumption of his complacent, superior manner of
the classroom toward the world at large. This defense is*

strengthened by a natural tendency toward a prim provincialism where practical present-day considerations are concerned (though he is most liberal—even radical—in his tolerant understanding of the manners and morals of Greece and Imperial Rome!). This classroom poise of his, however, he cannot quite carry off outside the classroom. There is an unconvincing quality about it that leaves his larger audience—and particularly the PROFESSOR *himself—subtly embarrassed. As* MARSDEN *is one of his old students, whom, in addition, he has known from childhood, he is perfectly at ease with him]*

MARSDEN

[*Holding out his hand—with unmistakable liking*]
Here I am again, Professor!

PROFESSOR LEEDS

[*Shaking his hand and patting him on the back—with genuine affection*]
So glad to see you, Charlie! A surprise, too! We didn't expect you back so soon!
[*He sits in his chair on the left of the table while* MARSDEN *sits in the rocker*]
[*Looking away from* MARSDEN *a moment, his face now full of selfish relief as he thinks*]
Fortunate, his coming back . . . always calming influence on Nina . . .

MARSDEN

And I never dreamed of returning so soon. But Europe, Professor, is the big casualty they were afraid to set down on the list.

PROFESSOR LEEDS

[*His face clouding*]

Yes, I suppose you found everything completely changed
since before the war.

[*He thinks resentfully*]

The war . . . Gordon! . . .

MARSDEN

Europe has "gone west"—

[*He smiles whimsically*]

to America, let's hope!

[*Then frowningly*]

I couldn't stand it.   There were millions sitting up with the
corpse already, who had a family right to be there—

[*Then matter-of-factly*]

I was wasting my time, too.   I couldn't write a line.

[*Then gaily*]

But where's Nina?   I must see Nina!

PROFESSOR LEEDS

She'll be right in.   She said she wanted to finish thinking
something out—   You'll find Nina changed, Charlie, greatly
changed!

[*He sighs—thinking with a trace of guilty alarm*]

The first thing she said at breakfast . . . "I dreamed of
Gordon" . . . as if she wanted to taunt me! . . . how
absurd! . . . her eyes positively glared! . . .

[*Suddenly blurting out resentfully*]

She dreams about Gordon.

MARSDEN

[*Looking at him with amused surprise*]

Well, I'd hardly call that a change, would you?

PROFESSOR LEEDS

[*Thinking, oblivious to this remark*]

But I must constantly bear in mind that she's not her-self . . . that she's a sick girl . . .

MARSDEN

[*Thinking*]

The morning news of Gordon's death came . . . her face like gray putty . . . beauty gone . . . no face can afford intense grief . . . it's only later when sorrow . . .

[*With concern*]

Just what do you mean by changed, Professor? Before I left she seemed to be coming out of that horrible numbed calm.

PROFESSOR LEEDS

[*Slowly and carefully*]

Yes, she has played a lot of golf and tennis this summer, motored around with her friends, and even danced a good deal. And she eats with a ravenous appetite.

[*Thinking frightenedly*]

Breakfast . . . "dreamed of Gordon" . . . what a look of hate for me in her eyes! . . .

MARSDEN

But that sounds splendid! When I left she wouldn't see anyone or go anywhere.

[*Thinking pityingly*]

Wandering from room to room . . . her thin body and pale lost face . . . gutted, love-abandoned eyes! . . .

PROFESSOR LEEDS

Well, now she's gone to the opposite extreme! Sees every-one—bores, fools—as if she'd lost all discrimination or wish

to discriminate.   And she talks interminably, Charlie—intentional nonsense, one would say!   Refuses to be serious!
Jeers at everything!

MARSDEN

[*Consolingly*]
Oh, that's all undoubtedly part of the effort she's making to
forget.

PROFESSOR LEEDS

[*Absent-mindedly*]
Yes.

[*Arguing with himself*]
Shall I tell him? . . . no . . . it might sound silly . . .
but it's terrible to be so alone in this . . . if Nina's
mother had lived . . . my wife . . . dead! . . . and for
a time I actually felt released! . . . wife! . . . helpmeet! . . . now I need help! . . . no use! . . . she's
gone! . . .

MARSDEN

[*Watching him—thinking with a condescending affection*]
Good little man . . . he looks worried . . . always fuss-
ing about something . . . he must get on Nina's
nerves. . . .
[*Reassuringly*]
No girl could forget Gordon in a hurry, especially after
the shock of his tragic death.

PROFESSOR LEEDS

[*Irritably*]
I realize that.
[*Thinking resentfully*]
Gordon . . . always Gordon with everyone! . . .

MARSDEN

By the way, I located the spot near Sedan where Gordon's machine fell. Nina asked me to, you know.

PROFESSOR LEEDS
[*Irritated—expostulatingly*]
For heaven's sake, don't remind her! Give her a chance to forget if you want to see her well again. After all, Charlie, life must be lived and Nina can't live with a corpse forever!
[*Trying to control his irritation and talk in an objective tone*]
You see, I'm trying to see things through clearly and unsentimentally. If you'll remember, I was as broken up as anyone over Gordon's death. I'd become so reconciled to Nina's love for him—although, as you know, I was opposed at first, and for fair reasons, I think, for the boy, for all his good looks and prowess in sport and his courses, really came of common people and had no money of his own except as he made a career for himself.

MARSDEN
[*A trifle defensively*]
I'm sure he would have had a brilliant career.

PROFESSOR LEEDS
[*Impatiently*]
No doubt. Although you must acknowledge, Charlie, that college heroes rarely shine brilliantly in after life. Unfortunately, the tendency to spoil them in the university is a poor training—

MARSDEN
But Gordon was absolutely unspoiled, I should say.

PROFESSOR LEEDS

[*Heatedly*]

Don't misunderstand me, Charlie! I'd be the first to acknowledge—

[*A bit pathetically*]

It isn't Gordon, Charlie. It's his memory, his ghost, you
might call it, haunting Nina, whose influence I have come to
dread because of the terrible change in her attitude toward
me.

[*His face twitches as if he were on the verge of tears—
he thinks desperately*]

I've got to tell him . . . he will see that I acted for the
best . . . that I was justified. . . .

[*He hesitates—then blurts out*]

It may sound incredible, but Nina has begun to act as if she
hated me!

MARSDEN

[*Startled*]

Oh, come now!

PROFESSOR LEEDS

[*Insistently*]

Absolutely! I haven't wanted to admit it. I've refused to
believe it, until it's become too appallingly obvious in her
whole attitude toward me!

[*His voice trembles*]

MARSDEN

[*Moved—expostulating*]

Oh, now you're becoming morbid! Why, Nina has always
idolized you! What possible reason—?

PROFESSOR LEEDS

[*Quickly*]

I can answer that, I think. She has a reason. But why she should blame me when she must know I acted for the best— You probably don't know, but just before he sailed for the front Gordon wanted their marriage to take place, and Nina consented. In fact, from the insinuations she lets drop now, she must have been most eager, but at the time— However, I felt it was ill-advised and I took Gordon aside and pointed out to him that such a precipitate marriage would be unfair to Nina, and scarcely honorable on his part.

MARSDEN

[*Staring at him wonderingly*]

You said that to Gordon?

[*Thinking cynically*]

A shrewd move! . . . Gordon's proud spot, fairness and honor! . . . but was it honorable of you? . . .

PROFESSOR LEEDS

[*With a touch of asperity*]

Yes, I said it, and I gave him my reason. There *was* the possibility he might be killed, in the flying service rather more than a possibility, which needless to say, I did not point out, but which Gordon undoubtedly realized, poor boy! If he were killed, he would be leaving Nina a widow, perhaps with a baby, with no resources, since he was penniless, except what pension she might get from the government; and all this while she was still at an age when a girl, especially one of Nina's charm and beauty, should have all of life before her. Decidedly, I told him, in justice to Nina, they must wait until he had come back and begun to establish his position in the world. That was the square thing. And Gordon was quick to agree with me!

MARSDEN

[*Thinking*]
The square thing! . . . but we must all be crooks where happiness is concerned! . . . steal or starve! . . .
[*Then rather ironically*]
And so Gordon told Nina he'd suddenly realized it wouldn't be fair to her. But I gather he didn't tell her it was your scruple originally?

PROFESSOR LEEDS

No, I asked him to keep what I said strictly confidential.

MARSDEN

[*Thinking ironically*]
Trusted to his honor again! . . . old fox! . . . poor Gordon! . . .
But Nina suspects now that you—?

PROFESSOR LEEDS

[*Startled*]
Yes. That's exactly it. She knows in some queer way. And she acts toward me exactly as if she thought I had deliberately destroyed her happiness, that I had hoped for Gordon's death and been secretly overjoyed when the news came!
[*His voice is shaking with emotion*]
And there you have it, Charlie—the whole absurd mess!
[*Thinking with a strident accusation*]
And it's true, you contemptible . . . !
[*Then miserably defending himself*]
No! . . . I acted unselfishly . . . for her sake! . . .

MARSDEN

[*Wonderingly*]

You don't mean to tell me she has accused you of all this?

PROFESSOR LEEDS

Oh, no, Charlie! Only by hints—looks—innuendos. She knows she has no real grounds, but in the present state of her mind the real and the unreal become confused—

MARSDEN

[*Thinking cynically*]
As always in all minds . . . or how could men live? . . .
[*Soothingly*]

That's just what you ought to bear in your mind—the state of hers—and not get so worked up over what I should say is a combination of imagination on both your parts.

[*He gets to his feet as he hears voices from the right*]

Buck up! This must be Nina coming.

[*The* PROFESSOR *gets to his feet, hastily composing his features into his bland, cultured expression*]

MARSDEN

[*Thinking self-mockingly but a bit worried about himself*]
My heart pounding! . . . seeing Nina again! . . . how sentimental . . . how she'd laugh if she knew! . . . and quite rightly . . . absurd for me to react as if I loved . . . that way . . . her dear old Charlie . . . ha! . . .
[*He smiles with bitter self-mockery*]

PROFESSOR LEEDS

[*Thinking worriedly*]
I hope she won't make a scene . . . she's seemed on the

verge all day . . . thank God, Charlie's like one of the
family . . . but what a life for me! . . . with the opening of the new term only a few weeks off! . . . I can't do
it . . . I'll have to call in a nerve specialist . . . but the
last one did her no good . . . his outrageous fee . . .
he can take it to court . . . I absolutely refuse . . . but
if he should bring suit? . . . what a scandal . . . no, I'll
have to pay . . . somehow . . . borrow . . . he has me
in a corner, the robber! . . .

NINA

[*Enters and stands just inside the doorway looking directly at her father with defiant eyes, her face set in an
expression of stubborn resolve. She is twenty, tall with
broad square shoulders, slim strong hips and long beauti-
fully developed legs—a fine athletic girl of the swimmer,
tennis player, golfer type. Her straw-blond hair, fram-
ing her sunburned face, is bobbed. Her face is striking,
handsome rather than pretty, the bone structure promi-
nent, the forehead high, the lips of her rather large mouth
clearly modelled above the firm jaw. Her eyes are beautiful and bewildering, extraordinarily large and a deep
greenish blue. Since* GORDON's *death they have a quality
of continually shuddering before some terrible enigma, of
being wounded to their depths and made defiant and resentful by their pain. Her whole manner, the charged
atmosphere she gives off, is totally at variance with her
healthy outdoor physique. It is strained, nerve-racked,
hectic, a terrible tension of will alone maintaining self-
possession. She is dressed in smart sport clothes. Too
preoccupied with her resolve to remember or see* MARS-
DEN, *she speaks directly to her father in a voice tensely
cold and calm*]
I have made up my mind, Father.

PROFESSOR LEEDS

[*Thinking distractedly*]
What does she mean? . . . oh, God help me! . . .
[*Flustered—hastily*]
Don't you see Charlie, Nina?

MARSDEN

[*Troubled—thinking*]
She has changed . . . what has happened? . . .
[*He comes forward toward her—a bit embarrassed but affectionately using his pet name for her*]
Hello, Nina Cara Nina! Are you trying to cut me dead, young lady?

NINA

[*Turning her eyes to* MARSDEN, *holding out her hand for him to shake, in her cool, preoccupied voice*]
Hello, Charlie.
[*Her eyes immediately return to her father*]
Listen, Father!

MARSDEN

[*Standing near her, concealing his chagrin*]
That hurts! . . . I mean nothing! . . . but she's a sick girl . . . I must make allowance . . .

PROFESSOR LEEDS

[*Thinking distractedly*]
That look in her eyes! . . . hate! . . .
[*With a silly giggle*]
Really, Nina, you're absolutely rude! What has Charlie done?

NINA

[*In her cool tone*]

Why, nothing. Nothing at all.

[*She goes to him with a detached, friendly manner*]

Did I seem rude, Charlie? I didn't mean to be.

[*She kisses him with a cool, friendly smile*]

Welcome home.

[*Thinking wearily*]

What has Charlie done? . . . nothing . . . and never will . . . Charlie sits beside the fierce river, immaculately timid, cool and clothed, watching the burning, frozen naked swimmers drown at last. . . .

MARSDEN

[*Thinking torturedly*]

Cold lips . . . the kiss of contempt! . . . for dear old Charlie! . . .

[*Forcing a good-natured laugh*]

Rude? Not a bit!

[*Banteringly*]

As I've often reminded you, what can I expect when the first word you ever spoke in this world was an insult to me. "Dog" you said, looking right at me—at the age of one!

[*He laughs. The* PROFESSOR *laughs nervously.* NINA *smiles perfunctorily*]

NINA

[*Thinking wearily*]

The fathers laugh at little daughter Nina . . . I must get away! . . . nice Charlie doggy . . . faithful . . . fetch and carry . . . bark softly in books at the deep night. . . .

PROFESSOR LEEDS

[*Thinking*]

What is she thinking? . . . I can't stand living like this! . . .

[*Giggle gone to a twitching grin*]

You are a cool one, Nina! You'd think you'd just seen Charlie yesterday!

NINA

[*Slowly—coolly and reflectively*]

Well, the war is over. Coming back safe from Europe isn't such an unusual feat now, is it?

MARSDEN

[*Thinking bitterly*]

A taunt . . . I didn't fight . . . physically unfit . . . not like Gordon . . . Gordon in flames . . . how she must resent my living! . . . thinking of me, scribbling in press bureau . . . louder and louder lies . . . drown the guns and the screams . . . deafen the world with lies . . . hired choir of liars! . . .

[*Forcing a joking tone*]

Little you know the deadly risks I ran, Nina! If you'd eaten some of the food they gave me on my renovated transport, you'd shower me with congratulations!

[*The* PROFESSOR *forces a snicker*]

NINA

[*Coolly*]

Well, you're here, and that's that.

[*Then suddenly expanding in a sweet, genuinely affectionate smile*]

And I *am* glad, Charlie, always glad you're here! You know that.

MARSDEN

[*Delighted and embarrassed*]

I hope so, Nina!

NINA

[*Turning on her father—determinedly*]

I must finish what I started to say, Father. I've thought it all out and decided that I simply must get away from here at once—or go crazy! And I'm going on the nine-forty to-night.

[*She turns to* MARSDEN *with a quick smile*]

You'll have to help me pack, Charlie!

[*Thinking with weary relief*]

Now that's said . . . I'm going . . . never come back . . . oh, how I loathe this room! . . .

MARSDEN

[*Thinking with alarm*]

What's this? . . . going? . . . going to whom? . . .

PROFESSOR LEEDS

[*Thinking—terrified*]

Going? . . . never come back to me? . . . no! . . .

[*Desperately putting on his prim severe manner toward an unruly pupil*]

This is rather a sudden decision, isn't it? You haven't mentioned before that you were considering—in fact, you've led me to believe that you were quite contented here—that is, of course I mean for the time being, and I really think—

MARSDEN

[*Looking at* NINA—*thinking with alarm*]

Going away to whom? . . .

[*Then watching the* PROFESSOR *with a pitying shudder*]
He's on the wrong tack with his professor's manner . . .
her eyes seeing cruelly through him . . . with what terrible recognition! . . . God, never bless me with children! . . .

NINA

[*Thinking with weary scorn*]
The Professor of Dead Languages is talking again . . .
a dead man lectures on the past of living . . . since
I was born I have been in his class, loving-attentive,
pupil-daughter Nina . . . my ears numb with spiritless
messages from the dead . . . dead words droning on
. . . listening because he is my cultured father . . . a
little more inclined to deafness than the rest (let me be
just) because he is my father . . . father? . . . what is
father? . . .

PROFESSOR LEEDS

[*Thinking—terrified*]
I must talk her out of it! . . . find the right words! . . .
oh, I know she won't hear me! . . . oh, wife, why did you
die, you would have talked to her, she would have listened
to you! . . .
[*Continuing in his professor's superior manner*]
—and I really think, in justice to yourself above all, you
ought to consider this step with great care before you definitely commit yourself. First and foremost, there is your
health to be taken into consideration. You've been very ill,
Nina, how perilously so perhaps you're not completely aware,
but I assure you, and Charlie can corroborate my statement,
that six months ago the doctors thought it might be years
before—and yet, by staying home and resting and finding
healthy outdoor recreation among your old friends, and

keeping your mind occupied with the routine of managing the household—

[*He forces a prim playful smile*]

and managing me, I might add!—you have wonderfully improved and I think it most ill-advised in the hottest part of August, while you're really still a convalescent—

NINA

[*Thinking*]

Talking! . . . his voice like a fatiguing dying tune droned on a beggar's organ . . . his words arising from the tomb of a soul in puffs of ashes . . .

[*Torturedly*]

Ashes! . . . oh, Gordon, my dear one! . . . oh, lips on my lips, oh, strong arms around me, oh, spirit so brave and generous and gay! . . . ashes dissolving into mud! . . . mud and ashes! . . . that's all! . . . gone! . . . gone forever from me! . . .

PROFESSOR LEEDS

[*Thinking angrily*]

Her eyes . . . I know that look . . . tender, loving . . . not for me . . . damn Gordon! . . . I'm glad he's dead! . . .

[*A touch of asperity in his voice*]

And at a couple of hours' notice to leave everything in the air, as it were—

[*Then judicially*]

No, Nina, frankly, I can't see it. You know I'd gladly consent to anything in the world to benefit you, but—surely, you can't have reflected!

NINA

[*Thinking torturedly*]
Gordon darling, I must go away where I can think of you
in silence! . . .
[*She turns on her father, her voice trembling with the
effort to keep it in control—icily*]
It's no use talking, Father. I *have* reflected and I am going!

PROFESSOR LEEDS

[*With asperity*]
But I tell you it's quite impossible! I don't like to bring
up the money consideration but I couldn't possibly afford—
And how will you support yourself, if I may ask? Two
years in the University, I am sorry to say, won't be much use
to you when applying for a job. And even if you had completely recovered from your nervous breakdown, which it's
obvious to anyone you haven't, then I most decidedly think
you should finish out your science course and take your
degree before you attempt—
[*Thinking desperately*]
No use! . . . she doesn't hear . . . thinking of Gordon
. . . she'll defy me . . .

NINA

[*Thinking desperately*]
I must keep calm . . . I mustn't let go or I'll tell him
everything . . . and I mustn't tell him . . . he's my
father . . .
[*With the same cold calculating finality*]
I've already had six months' training for a nurse. I will
finish my training. There's a doctor I know at a sanitarium

for crippled soldiers—a friend of Gordon's. I wrote to him and he answered that he'll gladly arrange it.

PROFESSOR LEEDS

[*Thinking furiously*]
Gordon's friend . . . Gordon again! . . .
[*Severely*]
You seriously mean to tell me you, in your condition, want to nurse in a soldiers' hospital! Absurd!

MARSDEN

[*Thinking with indignant revulsion*]
Quite right, Professor! . . . her beauty . . . all those men . . . in their beds . . . it's too revolting! . . .
[*With a persuasive quizzing tone*]
Yes, I must say I can't see you as a peace-time Florence Nightingale, Nina!

NINA

[*Coolly, struggling to keep control, ignoring these remarks*]
So you see, Father, I've thought of everything and there's not the slightest reason to worry about me. And I've been teaching Mary how to take care of you. So you won't need me at all. You can go along as if nothing had happened— and really, nothing will have happened that hasn't already happened.

PROFESSOR LEEDS

Why, even the manner in which you address me—the tone you take—proves conclusively that you're not yourself!

NINA

[*Her voice becoming a bit uncanny, her thoughts breaking through*]

No, I'm not myself yet. That's just it. Not all myself. But I've been becoming myself. And I must finish!

PROFESSOR LEEDS

[*With angry significance—to* MARSDEN]

You hear her, Charlie? She's a sick girl!

NINA

[*Slowly and strangely*]

I'm not sick. I'm too well. But they are sick and I must give my health to help them to live on, and to live on myself.

[*With a sudden intensity in her tone*]

I must pay for my cowardly treachery to Gordon! You should understand this, Father, you who—

[*She swallows hard, catching her breath*]

[*Thinking desperately*]

I'm beginning to tell him! . . . I mustn't! . . . he's my father! . . .

PROFESSOR LEEDS

[*In a panic of guilty fear, but defiantly*]

What do you mean? I am afraid you're not responsible for what you're saying.

NINA

[*Again with the strange intensity*]

I must pay! It's my plain duty! Gordon is dead! What

use is my life to me or anyone?   But I must make it of
use—by giving it!

[*Fiercely*]

I must learn to give myself, do you hear—give and give
until I can make that gift of myself for a man's happiness
without scruple, without fear, without joy except in his
joy!   When I've accomplished this I'll have found myself,
I'll know how to start in living my own life again!

[*Appealing to them with a desperate impatience*]

Don't you see?   In the name of the commonest decency and
honor, I owe it to Gordon!

PROFESSOR LEEDS

[*Sharply*]

No, I can't see—nor anyone else!

[*Thinking savagely*]

I hope Gordon is in hell! . . .

MARSDEN

[*Thinking*]

Give herself? . . . can she mean her body? . . . beautiful body . . . to cripples? . . . for Gordon's sake? . . .
damn Gordon! . . .

[*Coldly*]

What do you mean, you owe it to Gordon, Nina?

PROFESSOR LEEDS

[*Bitterly*]

Yes, how ridiculous!   It seems to me when you gave him
your love, he got more than he could ever have hoped—

NINA

[*With fierce self-contempt*]
I gave him? What did I give him? It's what I didn't give!
That last night before he sailed—in his arms until my body
ached—kisses until my lips were numb—knowing all that
night—something in me knowing he would die, that he would
never kiss me again—knowing this so surely yet with my
cowardly brain lying, no, he'll come back and marry you,
you'll be happy ever after and feel his children at your
breasts looking up with eyes so much like his, possessing eyes
so happy in possessing you!
[*Then violently*]
But Gordon never possessed me! I'm still Gordon's silly
virgin! And Gordon is muddy ashes! And I've lost my
happiness forever! All that last night I knew he wanted
me. I knew it was only the honorable code-bound Gordon,
who kept commanding from his brain, no, you mustn't, you
must respect her, you must wait till you have a marriage
license!
[*She gives a mocking laugh*]

PROFESSOR LEEDS

[*Shocked*]
Nina! This is really going too far!

MARSDEN

[*Repelled*]
[*With a superior sneer*]
Oh, come now, Nina! You've been reading books. Those
don't sound like your thoughts.

NINA

[*Without looking at him, her eyes on her father's—intensely*]

Gordon wanted me! I wanted Gordon! I should have made him take me! I knew he would die and I would have no children, that there would be no big Gordon or little Gordon left to me, that happiness was calling me, never to call again if I refused! And yet I did refuse! I didn't make him take me! I lost him forever! And now I am lonely and not pregnant with anything at all, but—but loathing!

[*She hurls this last at her father—fiercely*]

Why did I refuse? What was that cowardly something in me that cried, no, you mustn't, what would your father say?

PROFESSOR LEEDS

[*Thinking—furiously*]

What an animal! . . . and my daughter! . . . she doesn't get it from me! . . . was her mother like that? . . .

[*Distractedly*]

Nina! I really can't listen!

NINA

[*Savagely*]

And that's exactly what my father did say! Wait, he told Gordon! Wait for Nina till the war's over, and you've got a good job and can afford a marriage license!

PROFESSOR LEEDS

[*Crumbling pitifully*]

Nina! I—!

MARSDEN

[*Flurriedly—going to him*]
Don't take her seriously, Professor!

[*Thinking with nervous repulsion*]
Nina has changed . . . all flesh now . . . lust . . . who
would dream she was so sensual? . . . I wish I were out
of this! . . . I wish I hadn't come here today! . . .

NINA

[*Coldly and deliberately*]
Don't lie any more, Father! Today I've made up my mind
to face things. I know now why Gordon suddenly dropped
all idea of marriage before he left, how unfair to me he suddenly decided it would be! Unfair to me! Oh, that's humor-
ous! To think I might have had happiness, Gordon, and
now Gordon's child—

[*Then directly accusing him*]
You told him it'd be unfair, you put him on his honor,
didn't you?

PROFESSOR LEEDS

[*Collecting himself—woodenly*]
Yes. I did it for your sake, Nina.

NINA

[*In the same voice as before*]
It's too late for lies!

PROFESSOR LEEDS

[*Woodenly*]
Let us say then that I *persuaded* myself it was for your
sake. That may be true. You are young. You think one
can live with truth. Very well. It is also true I was jealous

of Gordon. I was alone and I wanted to keep your love. I
hated him as one hates a thief one may not accuse nor punish.
I did my best to prevent your marriage. I was glad when
he died. There. Is that what you wish me to say?

NINA

Yes. Now I begin to forget I've hated you. You were
braver than I, at least.

PROFESSOR LEEDS

I wanted to live comforted by your love until the end. In
short, I am a man who happens to be your father.
[*He hides his face in his hands and weeps softly*]
Forgive that man!

MARSDEN

[*Thinking timidly*]
In short, forgive us our possessing as we forgive those
who possessed before us . . . Mother must be wondering
what keeps me so long . . . it's time for tea . . . I must
go home . . .

NINA

[*Sadly*]
Oh, I forgive you. But do you understand now that I must
somehow find a way to give myself to Gordon still, that I
must pay my debt and learn to forgive myself?

PROFESSOR LEEDS

Yes.

NINA

Mary will look after you.

PROFESSOR LEEDS

Mary will do very well, I'm sure.

MARSDEN

[*Thinking*]
Nina has changed . . . this is no place for me . . .
Mother is waiting tea. . . .
[*Then venturing on an uncertain tone of pleasantry*]
Quite so, you two. But isn't this all nonsense? Nina will
be back with us in a month, Professor, what with the de-
pressing heat and humidity, and the more depressing halt
and the lame!

PROFESSOR LEEDS

[*Sharply*]
She must stay away until she gets well. This time I do
speak for her sake.

NINA

I'll take the nine-forty.
[*Turning to* MARSDEN— *with a sudden girlishness*]
Come on upstairs, Charlie, and help me pack!
[*She grabs him by the hand and starts to pull him away*]

MARSDEN

[*Shrugging his shoulders—confusedly*]
Well—I don't understand this!

NINA

[*With a strange smile*]
But some day I'll read it all in one of your books, Charlie,

and it'll be so simple and easy to understand that I won't
be able to recognize it, Charlie, let alone understand it!
> [*She laughs teasingly*]

Dear old Charlie!

MARSDEN

> [*Thinking in agony*]
> God damn in hell . . . dear old Charlie! . . .
> [*Then with a genial grin*]

I'll have to propose, Nina, if you continue to be my severest
critic! I'm a stickler for these little literary conventions,
you know!

NINA

All right. Propose while we pack.
> [*She leads him off, right*]

PROFESSOR LEEDS

> [*Blows his nose, wipes his eyes, sighs, clears his throat,
> squares his shoulders, pulls his coat down in front, sets his
> tie straight, and starts to take a brisk turn about the room.
> His face is washed blandly clean of all emotion*]

Three weeks now . . . new term . . . I will have to be
looking over my notes. . . .
> [*He looks out of window, front*]

Grass parched in the middle . . . Tom forgotten the
sprinkler . . . careless . . . ah, there goes Mr. Davis of
the bank . . . bank . . . my salary will go farther
now . . . books I really need . . . all bosh two can live
as cheaply as one . . . there are worse things than being
a trained nurse . . . good background of discipline . . .
she needs it . . . she may meet rich fellow there . . .
mature . . . only students here for her . . . and their
fathers never approve if they have anything. . . .
> [*He sits down with a forced sigh of peace*]

I am glad we had it out . . . his ghost will be gone
now . . . no more Gordon, Gordon, Gordon, love and
praise and tears, all for Gordon! . . . Mary will do very
well by me . . . I will have more leisure and peace of
mind . . . and Nina will come back home . . . when she
is well again . . . the old Nina! . . . my little Nina!
. . . she knows and she forgave me . . . she said so . . .
said! . . . but could she really? . . . don't you imagine?
. . . deep in her heart? . . . she still must hate? . . .
oh, God! . . . I feel cold! . . . alone! . . . this home is
abandoned! . . . the house is empty and full of death!
. . . there is a pain about my heart! . . .
[*He calls hoarsely, getting to his feet*]
Nina!

NINA S VOICE

[*Her voice, fresh and girlish, calls from upstairs*]
Yes, Father. Do you want me?

PROFESSOR LEEDS

[*Struggling with himself—goes to door and calls with
affectionate blandness*]
No. Never mind. Just wanted to remind you to call for a
taxi in good time.

NINA'S VOICE

I won't forget.

PROFESSOR LEEDS

[*Looks at his watch*]
Five-thirty just . . . nine-forty, the train . . . then . . .
Nina no more! . . . four hours more . . . she'll be
packing . . . then   good-bye . . . a   kiss . . . nothing
more ever to say to each other . . . and I'll die in here
some day . . . alone . . . gasp, cry out for help . . .
the president will speak at the funeral . . . Nina will be

here again . . . Nina in black . . . too late! . . .

[*He calls hoarsely*]

Nina!

[*There is no answer*]

In other room . . . doesn't hear . . . just as well . . .

[*He turns to the bookcase and pulls out the first volume his hands come on and opens it at random and begins to read aloud sonorously like a child whistling to keep up his courage in the dark*]

"Stetit unus in arcem

Erectus capitis victorque ad sidera mittit

Sidereos oculos propiusque adspectat Olympum

Inquiritque Iovem;" . . .

CURTAIN

ACT TWO

ACT TWO

SCENE: *The same as Scene One*, PROFESSOR LEEDS' *study.
It is about nine o'clock of a night in early fall, over a
year later. The appearance of the room is unchanged
except that all the shades, of the color of pale flesh,
are drawn down, giving the windows a suggestion
of lifeless closed eyes and making the room seem more
withdrawn from life than before. The reading lamp on
the table is lit. Everything on the table, papers, pencils,
pens, etc., is arranged in meticulous order.*
MARSDEN *is seated on the chair at center. He is
dressed carefully in an English made suit of blue serge
so dark as to seem black, and which, combined with the
gloomy brooding expression of his face, strongly sug-
gests one in mourning. His tall, thin body sags wearily
in the chair, his head is sunk forward, the chin almost
touching his chest, his eyes stare sadly at nothing.*

MARSDEN

[*His thoughts at ebb, without emphasis, sluggish and
melancholy*]
Prophetic Professor! . . . I remember he once said . . .
shortly after Nina went away . . . "some day, in here,
. . . you'll find me" . . . did he foresee? . . . no . . .
everything in life is so contemptuously accidental! . . .
God's sneer at our self-importance! . . .
[*Smiling grimly*]

47

Poor Professor! he was horribly lonely . . . tried to
hide it . . . always telling you how beneficial the train-
ing at the hospital would be for her . . . poor old
chap! . . .
[*His voice grows husky and uncertain—he controls it—
straightens himself*]
What time is it? . . .
[*He takes out his watch mechanically and looks at it*]
Ten after nine. . . . Nina ought to be here. . . .
[*Then with sudden bitterness*]
Will she feel any real grief over his death, I wonder? . . .
I doubt it! . . . but why am I so resentful? . . . the two
times I've visited the hospital she's been pleasant enough
. . . pleasantly evasive! . . . perhaps she thought her
father had sent me to spy on her . . . poor Professor!
. . . at least she answered his letters . . . he used to
show them to me . . . pathetically overjoyed . . .
newsy, loveless scripts, telling nothing whatever about
herself . . . well, she won't have to compose them any
more . . . she never answered mine . . . she might at
least have acknowledged them. . . . Mother thinks she's
behaved quite inexcusably . . .
[*Then jealously*]
I suppose every single damned inmate has fallen in love
with her! . . . her eyes seemed cynical . . . sick with
men . . . as though I'd looked into the eyes of a prosti-
tute . . . not that I ever have . . . except that once . . .
the dollar house . . . hers were like patent leather but-
tons in a saucer of blue milk! . . .
[*Getting up with a movement of impatience*]
The devil! . . . what beastly incidents our memories insist on cherishing! . . . the ugly and disgusting . . . the
beautiful things we have to keep diaries to remember!
. . .

[*He smiles with a wry amusement for a second—then bitterly*]

That last night Nina was here . . . she talked so brazenly about giving herself . . . I wish I knew the truth of what she's been doing in that house full of men . . . particularly that self-important young ass of a doctor! . . . Gordon's friend! . . .

[*He frowns at himself, determinedly puts an end to his train of thought and comes and sits down again in the chair—in sneering, conversational tones as if he were this time actually addressing another person*]

Really, it's hardly a decent time, is it, for that kind of speculation . . . with her father lying dead upstairs? . . .

[*A silence as if he had respectably squelched himself—then he pulls out his watch mechanically and stares at it. As he does so a noise of a car is heard approaching, stopping at the curb beyond the garden. He jumps to his feet and starts to go to door—then hesitates confusedly*]

No, let Mary go . . . I wouldn't know what to do . . . take her in my arms? . . . kiss her? . . . right now? . . . or wait until she? . . .

[*A bell rings insistently from the back of the house. From the front voices are heard, first* NINA'S, *then a man's.* MARSDEN *starts, his face suddenly angry and dejected*]

Someone with her! . . . a man! . . . I thought she'd be alone! . . .

[MARY *is heard shuffling to the front door which is opened. Immediately, as* MARY *sees* NINA, *she breaks down and there is the sound of her uncontrolled sobbing and choking, incoherent words drowning out* NINA'S *voice, soothing her*]

NINA

[*As* MARY'S *grief subsides a trifle, her voice is heard, flat and toneless*]
Isn't Mr. Marsden here, Mary?
[*She calls*]
Charlie!

MARSDEN

[*Confused—huskily*]
In here——I'm in the study, Nina.
[*He moves uncertainly toward the door*]

NINA

[*Comes in and stands just inside the doorway. She is dressed in a nurse's uniform with cap, a raglan coat over it. She appears older than in the previous scene, her face is pale and much thinner, her cheek bones stand out, her mouth is taut in hard lines of a cynical scorn. Her eyes try to armor her wounded spirit with a defensive stare of disillusionment. Her training has also tended to coarsen her fiber a trifle, to make her insensitive to suffering, to give her the nurse's professionally callous attitude. In her fight to regain control of her nerves she has over-striven after the cool and efficient poise, but she is really in a more highly strung, disorganized state than ever, although she is now more capable of suppressing and concealing it. She remains strikingly handsome and her physical appeal is enhanced by her pallor and the mysterious suggestion about her of hidden experience. She stares at* MARSDEN *blankly and speaks in queer flat tones*]
Hello, Charlie. He's dead, Mary says.

MARSDEN

[*Nodding his head several times—stupidly*]

Yes.

NINA

[*In same tones*]

It's too bad. I brought Doctor Darrell. I thought there
might be a chance.

[*She pauses and looks about the room*]
[*Thinking confusedly*]

His books . . . his chair . . . he always sat there . . .
there's his table . . . little Nina was never allowed to
touch anything . . . she used to sit on his lap . . . cud-
dle against him . . . dreaming into the dark beyond the
windows . . . warm in his arms before the fireplace . . .
dreams like sparks soaring up to die in the cold dark . . .
warm in his love, safe-drifting into sleep . . ."Daddy's
girl, aren't you?" . . .

[*She looks around and then up and down*]

His home . . . my home . . . he was my father . . .
he's dead . . .

[*She shakes her head*]

Yes, I hear you, little Nina, but I don't understand one
word of it. . . .

[*She smiles with a cynical self-contempt*]

I'm sorry, Father! . . . you see you've been dead for
me a long time . . . when Gordon died, all men died . . .
what did you feel for me then? . . . nothing . . . and
now I feel nothing . . . it's too bad . . .

MARSDEN

[*Thinking woundedly*]

I hoped she would throw herself in my arms . . . weeping . . . hide her face on my shoulder . . . "Oh,
Charlie, you're all I've got left in the world . . ."

[*Then angrily*]
Why did she have to bring that Darrell with her?

NINA

[*Flatly*]
When I said good-bye that night I had a premonition I'd
never see him again.

MARSDEN

[*Glad of this opening for moral indignation*]
You've never tried to see him, Nina!
[*Then overcome by disgust with himself—contritely*]
Forgive me! It was rotten of me to say that!

NINA

[*Shaking her head—flatly*]
I didn't want him to see what he would have thought was me.
[*Ironically*]
That's the other side of it you couldn't dissect into words
from here, Charlie!
[*Then suddenly asking a necessary question in her
nurse's cool, efficient tones*]
Is he upstairs?
[*Marsden nods stupidly*]
I'll take Ned up. I might as well.
[*She turns and walks out briskly*]

MARSDEN

[*Staring after her—dully*]
That isn't Nina. . . .
[*Indignantly*]
They've killed her soul down there! . . .
[*Tears come to his eyes suddenly and he pulls out his
handkerchief and wipes them, muttering huskily*]
Poor old Professor! . . .

[*Then suddenly jeering at himself*]

For God's sake, stop acting! . . . it isn't the Professor! . . . dear old Charlie is crying because she didn't weep on his shoulder . . . as he had hoped! . . .

[*He laughs harshly—then suddenly sees a man outside the doorway and stares—then calls sharply*]

Who's that?

EVANS

[*His voice embarrassed and hesitating comes from the hall*]

It's all right.

[*He appears in the doorway, grinning bashfully*]

It's me—I, I mean—Miss Leeds told me to come in here.

[*He stretches out his hand awkwardly*]

Guess you don't remember me, Mr. Marsden. Miss Leeds introduced us one day at the hospital. You were leaving just as I came in. Evans is my name.

MARSDEN

[*Who has been regarding him with waning resentment, forces a cordial smile and shakes hands*]

Oh, yes. At first I couldn't place you.

EVANS

[*Awkwardly*]

I sort of feel I'm butting in.

MARSDEN

[*Beginning to be taken by his likable boyish quality*]

Not at all. Sit down.

[*He sits in the rocker at center as* EVANS *goes to the bench at right*]

[EVANS *sits uncomfortably hunched forward, twiddling his hat in his hands. He is above the medium height, very blond, with guileless, diffident blue eyes, his figure inclined to immature lumbering outlines. His face is fresh and red-cheeked, handsome in a boyish fashion. His manner is bashful with women or older men, coltishly playful with his friends. There is a lack of self-confidence, a lost and strayed appealing air about him, yet with a hint of some unawakened obstinate force beneath his apparent weakness. Although he is twenty-five and has been out of college three years, he still wears the latest in collegiate clothes and as he looks younger than he is, he is always mistaken for an undergraduate and likes to be. It keeps him placed in life for himself*]

MARSDEN

[*Studying him keenly—amused*]
This is certainly no giant intellect . . . overgrown boy . . . likable quality though . . .

EVANS

[*Uneasy under* MARSDEN'S *eyes*]
Giving me the once-over . . . seems like good egg . . . Nina says he is . . . suppose I ought to say something about his books, but I can't even remember a title of one . . .
[*He suddenly blurts out*]
You've known Nina—Miss Leeds—ever since she was a kid, haven't you?

MARSDEN

[*A bit shortly*]
Yes. How long have you known her?

EVANS

Well—really only since she's been at the hospital, although
I met her once years ago at a Prom with Gordon Shaw.

MARSDEN

[*Indifferently*]
Oh, you knew Gordon?

EVANS

[*Proudly*]
Sure thing! I was in his class!
[*With admiration amounting to hero-worship*]
He sure was a wonder, wasn't he?

MARSDEN

[*Cynically*]
Gordon über alles and forever! . . . I begin to appreciate
the Professor's viewpoint . . .
[*Casually*]
A fine boy! Did you know him well?

EVANS

No. The crowd he went with were mostly fellows who were
good at sports—and I always was a dud.
[*Forcing a smile*]
I was always one of the first to get bounced off the squad
in any sport.
[*Then with a flash of humble pride*]
But I never quit trying, anyway!

MARSDEN

[*Consolingly*]
Well, the sport hero usually doesn't star after college.

EVANS

Gordon did!

> [*Eagerly—with intense admiration*]

In the war! He was an ace! And he always fought just
as cleanly as he'd played football! Even the Huns respected
him!

MARSDEN

> [*Thinking cynically*]
> This Gordon worshipper must be the apple of Nina's eye!
> . . .
> [*Casually*]

Were you in the army?

EVANS

> [*Shamefacedly*]

Yes—infantry—but I never got to the front—never saw
anything exciting.

> [*Thinking glumly*]
> Won't tell him I tried for flying service . . . wanted to
> get in Gordon's outfit . . . couldn't make the physical
> exam. . . . never made anything I wanted . . . suppose
> I'll lose out with Nina, too . . .
> [*Then rallying himself*]
> Hey, you! . . . what's the matter with you? . . . don't
> quit! . . .

MARSDEN

> [*Who has been staring at him inquisitively*]

How did you happen to come out here tonight?

EVANS

I was calling on Nina when your wire came. Ned thought
I better come along, too—might be of some use.

MARSDEN

[*Frowning*]
You mean Doctor Darrell?
[Evans *nods*]
Is he a close friend of yours?

EVANS

[*Hesitatingly*]
Well, sort of. Roomed in the same dorm with me at college.
He was a senior when I was a freshman. Used to help me
along in lots of ways. Took pity on me, I was so green.
Then about a year ago when I went to the hospital to visit
a fellow who'd been in my outfit I ran into him again.
[*Then with a grin*]
But I wouldn't say Ned was close to anyone. He's a dyed-
in-the-wool doc. He's only close to whatever's the matter
with you!
[*He chuckles—then hastily*]
But don't get me wrong about him. He's the best egg ever!
You know him, don't you?

MARSDEN

[*Stiffly*]
Barely. Nina introduced us once.
[*Thinking bitterly*]
He's upstairs alone with her . . . I hoped it would be
I who . . .

EVANS

Don't want him to get the wrong idea of Ned . . . Ned's
my best friend . . . doing all he can to help me with
Nina . . . he thinks she'll marry me in the end . . .
God, if she only would! . . . I wouldn't expect her to

love me at first . . . be happy only to take care of her
. . . cook her breakfast . . . bring it up to her in
bed . . . tuck the pillows behind her . . . comb her hair
for her . . . I'd be happy just to kiss her hair! . . .

MARSDEN

[*Agitated—thinking suspiciously*]
What are Darrell's relations with Nina? . . . close to
what's the matter with her? . . . damned thoughts! . . .
why should I care? . . . I'll ask this Evans . . . pump
him while I have a chance . . .
[*With forced indifference*]
Is your friend, the Doctor, "close" to Miss Leeds? She's
had quite a lot the matter with her since her breakdown, if
that's what interests him!
[*He smiles casually*]

EVANS

[*Gives a start, awakening from his dream*]
Oh—er—yes. He's always trying to bully her into taking
better care of herself, but she only laughs at him.
[*Soberly*]
It'd be much better if she'd take his advice.

MARSDEN

[*Suspiciously*]
No doubt.

EVANS

[*Pronounces with boyish solemnity*]
She isn't herself, Mr. Marsden. And I think nursing all
those poor guys keeps the war before her when she ought to
forget it. She ought to give up nursing and be nursed for
a change, that's my idea.

MARSDEN

[*Struck by this—eagerly*]
Exactly my opinion.
[*Thinking*]
If she'd settle down here . . . I could come over every
day . . . I'd nurse her . . . Mother home . . . Nina
here . . . how I could work then! . . .

EVANS

[*Thinking*]
He certainly seems all for me . . . so far! . . .
[*Then in a sudden flurry*]
Shall I tell him? . . . he'll be like her guardian now . . .
I've got to know how he stands . . .
[*He starts with a solemn earnestness*]
Mr. Marsden, I—there's something I ought to tell you, I
think. You see, Nina's talked a lot about you. I know how
much she thinks of you. And now her old man—
[*He hesitates in confusion*]
I mean, her father's dead—

MARSDEN

[*In a sort of panic—thinking*]
What's this? . . . proposal? . . . in form? . . . for her
hand? . . . to me? . . . Father Charlie now, eh? . . .
ha! . . . God, what a fool! . . . does he imagine she'd
ever love him? . . . but she might . . . not bad looking
. . . likable, innocent . . . something to mother . . .

EVANS

[*Blundering on regardless now*]
I know it's hardly the proper time—

MARSDEN

[*Interrupting—dryly*]

Perhaps I can anticipate. You want to tell me you're in love with Nina?

EVANS

Yes, sir, and I've asked her to marry me.

MARSDEN

What did she say?

EVANS

[*Sheepishly*]

Nothing. She just smiled.

MARSDEN

[*With relief*]

Ah.

[*Then harshly*]

Well, what could you expect? Surely you must know she still loves Gordon?

EVANS

[*Manfully*]

Sure I know it—and I admire her for it! Most girls forget too easily. She ought to love Gordon for a long time yet. And I know I'm an awful wash-out compared to him—but I love her as much as he did, or anyone could! And I'll work my way up for her—I know I can!—so I can give her everything she wants. And I wouldn't ask for anything in return except the right to take care of her.

[*Blurts out confusedly*]

I never think of her—that way—she's too beautiful and

wonderful—not that I don't hope she'd come to love me in time—

MARSDEN

[Sharply]
And just what do you expect me to do about all this?

EVANS

[Taken aback]
Why—er—nothing, sir. I just thought you ought to know.
[Sheepishly he glances up at ceiling, then down at floor, twiddling his hat]

MARSDEN

[Thinking—at first with a grudging appreciation and envy]
He thinks he means that . . . pure love! . . . it's easy to talk . . . he doesn't know life . . . but he might be good for Nina . . . if she were married to this simpleton would she be faithful? . . . and then I? . . . what a vile thought! . . . I don't mean that! . . .
[Then forcing a kindly tone]
You see, there's really nothing I can do about it.
[With a smile]
If Nina will, she will—and if she won't, she won't. But I can wish you good luck.

EVANS

[Immediately all boyish gratitude]
Thanks! That's darn fine of you, Mr. Marsden!

MARSDEN

But I think we'd better let the subject drop, don't you?
We're forgetting that her father—

EVANS

[*Guiltily embarrassed*]

Yes—sure—I'm a damn fool! Excuse me!

[*There is the noise of steps from the hall and* DOCTOR
EDMUND DARRELL *enters. He is twenty-seven, short,
dark, wiry, his movements rapid and sure, his manner
cool and observant, his dark eyes analytical. His head is
handsome and intelligent. There is a quality about him,
provoking and disturbing to women, of intense passion
which he has rigidly trained himself to control and set
free only for the objective satisfaction of studying his
own and their reactions; and so he has come to consider
himself as immune to love through his scientific understanding of its real sexual nature. He sees* EVANS *and*
MARSDEN, *nods at* MARSDEN *silently, who returns it coldly,
goes to the table and taking a prescription pad from his
pocket, hastily scratches on it*]

MARSDEN

[*Thinking sneeringly*]

Amusing, these young doctors! . . . perspire with the effort to appear cool! . . . writing a prescription . . .
cough medicine for the corpse, perhaps! . . . good-look-
ing? . . . more or less . . . attractive to women, I dare
say. . . .

DARRELL

[*Tears it off—hands it to* EVANS]

Here, Sam. Run along up the street and get this filled.

EVANS

[*With relief*]

Sure. Glad of the chance for a walk.

[*He goes out, rear*]

DARRELL

[*Turning to Marsden*]

It's for Nina. She's got to get some sleep tonight.

[*He sits down abruptly in the chair at center.* MARSDEN *unconsciously takes the* PROFESSOR'S *place behind the table. The two men stare at each other for a moment,* DARRELL *with a frank probing, examining look that ruffles* MARSDEN *and makes him all the more resentful toward him*]

This Marsden doesn't like me . . . that's evident . . . but he interests me . . . read his books . . . wanted to know his bearing on Nina's case . . . his novels just well-written surface . . . no depth, no digging underneath . . . why? . . . has the talent but doesn't dare . . . afraid he'll meet himself somewhere . . . one of those poor devils who spend their lives trying not to discover which sex they belong to! . . .

MARSDEN

Giving me the fishy, diagnosing eye they practice at medical school . . . like freshmen from Ioway cultivating broad A's at Harvard! . . . what is his specialty? . . . neurologist, I think . . . I hope not psychoanalyst . . . a lot to account for, Herr Freud! . . . punishment to fit his crimes, be forced to listen eternally during breakfast while innumerable plain ones tell him dreams about snakes . . . pah, what an easy cure-all! . . . sex the philosopher's stone . . . "O Oedipus, O my king! The world is adopting you!" . . .

DARRELL

Must pitch into him about Nina . . . have to have his help . . . damn little time to convince him . . . he's the kind you have to explode a bomb under to get them to

move . . . but not too big a bomb . . . they blow to
pieces easily . . .

[*Brusquely*]

Nina's gone to pot again! Not that her father's death is a
shock in the usual sense of grief. I wish to God it were! No,
it's a shock because it's finally convinced her she can't feel
anything any more. That's what she's doing upstairs now—
trying to goad herself into feeling something!

MARSDEN

[*Resentfully*]

I think you're mistaken. She loved her father—

DARRELL

[*Shortly and dryly*]

We can't waste time being sentimental, Marsden! She'll
be down any minute, and I've got a lot to talk over with you.

[*As* MARSDEN *seems again about to protest*]

Nina has a real affection for you and I imagine you have
for her. Then you'll want as much as I do to get her
straightened out. She's a corking girl. She ought to have
every chance for a happy life.

[*Then sharply driving his words in*]

But the way she's conditioned now, there's no chance. She's
piled on too many destructive experiences. A few more and
she'll dive for the gutter just to get the security that comes
from knowing she's touched bottom and there's no farther
to go!

MARSDEN

[*Revolted and angry, half-springs to his feet*]

Look here, Darrell, I'll be damned if I'll listen to such a
ridiculous statement!

DARRELL

[*Curtly—with authority*]

How do you know it's ridiculous? What do you know of Nina since she left home? But she hadn't been nursing with us three days before I saw she really ought to be a patient; and ever since then I've studied her case. So I think it's up to you to listen.

MARSDEN

[*Freezingly*]

I'm listening.

[*With apprehensive terror*]

Gutter . . . has she . . . I wish he wouldn't tell me! . . .

DARRELL

[*Thinking*]

How much need I tell him? . . . can't tell him the raw truth about her promiscuity . . . he isn't built to face reality . . . no writer is outside of his books . . . have to tone it down for him . . . but not too much! . . .

Nina has been giving way more and more to a morbid longing for martyrdom. The reason for it is obvious. Gordon went away without—well, let's say marrying her. The war killed him. She was left suspended. Then she began to blame herself and to want to sacrifice herself and at the same time give happiness to various fellow war-victims by pretending to love them. It's a pretty idea but it hasn't worked out. Nina's a bad actress. She hasn't convinced the men of her love—or herself of her good intentions. And each experience of this kind has only left her more a prey to a guilty conscience than before and more determined to punish herself!

MARSDEN

[*Thinking*]

What does he mean? . . . how far did she? . . . how many? . . .

[*Coldly and sneeringly*]

May I ask on what specific actions of hers this theory of yours is based?

DARRELL

[*Coldly in turn*]

On her evident craving to make an exhibition of kissing, necking, petting—whatever you call it—spooning in general—with any patient in the institution who got a case on her!

[*Ironically—thinking*]

Spooning! . . . rather a mild word for her affairs . . . but strong enough for this ladylike soul. . . .

MARSDEN

[*Bitterly*]

He's lying! . . . what's he trying to hide? . . . was he one of them? . . . her lover? . . . I must get her away from him . . . get her to marry Evans! . . .

[*With authority*]

Then she mustn't go back to your hospital, that's certain!

DARRELL

[*Quickly*]

You're quite right. And that brings me to what I want you to urge her to do.

MARSDEN

[*Thinking suspiciously*]

He doesn't want her back . . . I must have been

wrong . . . but there might be many reasons why he'd
wish to get rid of her . . . .

[*Coldly*]

I think you exaggerate my influence.

DARRELL

[*Eagerly*]

Not a bit. You're the last link connecting her with the girl
she used to be before Gordon's death. You're closely as-
sociated in her mind with that period of happy security, of
health and peace of mind. I know that from the way she
talks about you. You're the only person she still respects—
and really loves.

[*As* MARSDEN *starts guiltily and glances at him in confusion—with a laugh*]

Oh, you needn't look frightened. I mean the sort of love
she'd feel for an uncle.

MARSDEN

[*Thinking in agony*]

Frightened? . . . was I? . . . only person she loves . . .
and then he said "love she'd feel for an uncle" . . .
Uncle Charlie now! . . . God damn him! . . .

DARRELL

[*Eyeing him*]

Looks damnably upset . . . wants to evade all responsibility for her, I suppose . . . he's that kind . . . all the
better! . . . he'll be only too anxious to get her safely
married. . . .

[*Bluntly*]

And that's why I've done all this talking. You've got to
help snap her out of this.

MARSDEN

[*Bitterly*]
And how, if I may ask?

DARRELL

There's only one way I can see.   Get her to marry Sam
Evans.

MARSDEN

[*Astonished*]
Evans?
[*He makes a silly gesture toward the door*]
[*Thinking confusedly*]
Wrong again . . . why does he want her married to . . .
it's some trick. . . .

DARRELL

Yes, Evans.   He's in love with her.   And it's one of those
unselfish loves you read about.   And she is fond of him.   In
a maternal way, of course—but that's just what she needs
now, someone she cares about to mother and boss and keep
her occupied.   And still more important, this would give her
a chance to have children.   She's got to find normal outlets
for her craving for sacrifice.   She needs normal love objects
for the emotional life Gordon's death blocked up in her.   Now
marrying Sam ought to do the trick.   Ought to.   Naturally, no one can say for certain.   But I think his unselfish
love, combined with her real liking for him, will gradually
give her back a sense of security and a feeling of being worth
something to life again, and once she's got that, she'll be
saved!

[*He has spoken with persuasive feeling. He asks anxiously*]
Doesn't that seem good sense to you?

MARSDEN

[*Suspicious—dryly non-committal*]
I'm sorry but I'm in no position to say. I don't know anything about Evans, for one thing.

DARRELL

[*Emphatically*]
Well, I do. He's a fine healthy boy, clean and unspoiled.
You can take my word for that. And I'm convinced he's
got the right stuff in him to succeed, once he grows up and
buckles down to work. He's only a big kid now, but all he
needs is a little self-confidence and a sense of responsibility.
He's holding down a fair job, too, considering he's just
started in the advertising game—enough to keep them
living.
[*With a slight smile*]
I'm prescribing for Sam, too, when I boost this wedding.

MARSDEN

[*His snobbery coming out*]
Do you know his family—what sort of people?—

DARRELL

[*Bitingly*]
I'm not acquainted with their social qualifications, if that's
what you mean! They're upstate country folks—fruit

growers and farmers, well off, I believe. Simple, healthy
people, I'm sure of that although I've never met them.

MARSDEN

[*A bit shamefacedly—changing the subject hastily*]
Have you suggested this match to Nina?

DARRELL

Yes, a good many times lately in a half-joking way. If I
were serious she wouldn't listen, she'd say I was prescribing.
But I think what I've said has planted it in her mind as a
possibility.

MARSDEN

[*Thinking suspiciously*]
Is this Doctor her lover? . . . trying to pull the wool
over my eyes? . . . use me to arrange a convenient tri-
angle for him? . . .
[*Harshly—but trying to force a joking tone*]
Do you know what I'm inclined to suspect, Doctor? That
you may be in love with Nina yourself!

DARRELL

[*Astonished*]
The deuce you do! What in the devil makes you think that?
Not that any man mightn't fall in love with Nina. Most of
them do. But I didn't happen to. And what's more I never
could. In my mind she always belongs to Gordon. It's
probably a reflection of her own silly fixed idea about him.
[*Suddenly, dryly and harshly*]
And I couldn't share a woman—even with a ghost!
[*Thinking cynically*]

Not to mention the living who have had her! . . . Sam
doesn't know about them . . . and I'll bet he couldn't
believe it of her even if she confessed! . . .

MARSDEN

[*Thinking baffledly*]
Wrong again! . . . he isn't lying . . . but I feel he's
hiding something . . . why does he speak so resentfully
of Gordon's memory? . . . why do I sympathize? . . .
[*In a strange mocking ironic tone*]
I can quite appreciate your feeling about Gordon. I wouldn't
care to share with a ghost-lover myself. That species of
dead is so invulnerably alive! Even a doctor couldn't kill
one, eh?
[*He forces a laugh—then in a friendly confidential tone*]
Gordon is too egregious for a ghost. That was the way
Nina's father felt about him, too.
[*Suddenly reminded of the dead man—in penitently sad
tones*]
You didn't know her father, did you? A charming old fellow!

DARRELL

[*Hearing a noise from the hall—warningly*]
Sstt!
[NINA *enters slowly. She looks from one to the other
with a queer, quick, inquisitive stare, but her face is a pale
expressionless mask drained of all emotional response to
human contacts. It is as if her eyes were acting on their
own account as restless, prying, recording instruments.
The two men have risen and stare at her anxiously.
DARRELL moves back and to one side until he is standing
in relatively the same place as* MARSDEN *had occupied*

in the previous scene while MARSDEN *is in her father's place and she stops where she had been. There is a pause. Then just as each of the men is about to speak, she answers as if they had asked a question*]

NINA

[*In a queer flat voice*]

Yes, he's dead—my father—whose passion created me—who began me—he is ended. There is only his end living—his death. It lives now to draw nearer me, to draw me nearer, to become my end!

[*Then with a strange twisted smile*]

How we poor monkeys hide from ourselves behind the sounds called words!

MARSDEN

[*Thinking frightenedly*]

How terrible she is! . . . who is she? . . . not my Nina! . . .

[*As if to reassure himself—timidly*]

Nina!

[DARRELL *makes an impatient gesture for him to let her go on. What she is saying interests him and he feels talking it out will do her good. She looks at* MARSDEN *for a moment startledly as if she couldn't recognize him*]

NINA

What?

[*Then placing him—with real affection that is like a galling goad to him*]

Dear old Charlie!

MARSDEN

Dear damned Charlie! . . . She loves to torture! . . .
[*Then forcing a smile—soothingly*]
Yes, Nina Cara Nina! Right here!

NINA

[*Forcing a smile*]
You look frightened, Charlie. Do I seem queer? It's because I've suddenly seen the lies in the sounds called words.
You know—grief, sorrow, love, father—those sounds our
lips make and our hands write. You ought to know what
I mean. You work with them. Have you written another
novel lately? But, stop to think, you're just the one who
couldn't know what I mean. With you the lies have become
the only truthful things. And I suppose that's the logical
conclusion to the whole evasive mess, isn't it? Do you understand me, Charlie? Say lie—
[*She says it, drawing it out*]
L-i-i-e! Now say life. L-i-i-f-e! You see! Life is just
a long drawn out lie with a sniffling sigh at the end!
[*She laughs*]

MARSDEN

[*In strange agony*]
She's hard! . . . like a whore! . . . tearing your heart
with dirty finger nails! . . . my Nina! . . . cruel bitch!
. . . some day I won't bear it! . . . I'll scream out the
truth about every woman! . . . no kinder at heart than
dollar tarts! . . .
[*Then in a passion of remorse*]
Forgive me, Mother! . . . I didn't mean all! . . .

DARRELL

[*A bit worried himself now—persuasively*]

Why not sit down, Nina, and let us two gentlemen sit down?

NINA

[*Smiling at him swiftly and mechanically*]

Oh, all right, Ned.

[*She sits at center. He comes and sits on the bench.*
MARSDEN *sits by the table. She continues sarcastically*]

Are you prescribing for me again, Ned? This is my pet doctor, Charlie. He couldn't be happy in heaven unless God called him in because He'd caught something! Did you ever know a young scientist, Charlie? He believes if you pick a lie to pieces, the pieces are the truth! I like him because he's so inhuman. But once he kissed me—in a moment of carnal weakness! I was as startled as if a mummy had done it! And then he looked so disgusted with himself! I had to laugh!

[*She smiles at him with a pitying scorn*]

DARRELL

[*Good-naturedly smiling*]

That's right! Rub it in!

[*Ruffled but amused in spite of it*]

I'd forgotten about that kiss . . . I was sore at myself afterwards . . . she was so damned indifferent! . . ..

NINA

[*Wanderingly*]

Do you know what I was doing upstairs? I was trying to pray. I tried hard to pray to the modern science God. I thought of a million light years to a spiral nebula—one other universe among innumerable others. But how could that God care about our trifling misery of death-born-of-birth? I couldn't believe in Him, and I wouldn't if I could! I'd rather imitate His indifference and prove I had that one trait at least in common!

MARSDEN

[*Worriedly*]
Nina, why don't you lie down?

NINA

[*Jeeringly*]
Oh, let me talk, Charlie! They're only words, remember! So many many words have jammed up into thoughts in my poor head! You'd better let them overflow or they'll burst the dam! I wanted to believe in any God at any price—a heap of stones, a mud image, a drawing on a wall, a bird, a fish, a snake, a baboon—or even a good man preaching the simple platitudes of truth, those Gospel words we love the sound of but whose meaning we pass on to spooks to live by!

MARSDEN

[*Again—half-rising—frightenedly*]
Nina! You ought to stop talking. You'll work yourself into—
[*He glances angrily at Darrell as if demanding that, as a doctor, he do something*]

NINA

[*With bitter hopelessness*]

Oh, all right!

DARRELL

[*Answering his look—thinking*]

You poor fool! . . . it'll do her good to talk this out of
her system . . . and then it'll be up to you to bring her
around to Sam . . .

[*Starts toward the door*]

Think I'll go out and stretch my legs.

MARSDEN

[*Thinking—in a panic*]

I don't want to be alone with her! . . . I don't know
her! . . . I'm afraid! . . .

[*Protestingly*]

Well—but—hold on—I'm sure Nina would rather—

NINA

[*Dully*]

Let him go. I've said everything I can ever say—to him.
I want to talk to you, Charlie.

[*Darrell goes out noiselessly with a meaning look at
Marsden—a pause*]

MARSDEN

[*Thinking tremblingly*]

Here . . . now . . . what I hoped . . . she and I alone
. . . she will cry . . . I will comfort her . . . why am
I so afraid? . . . whom do I fear? . . . is it she? . . .
or I? . . .

NINA

[*Suddenly, with pity yet with scorn*]

Why have you always been so timid, Charlie? Why are you always afraid? What are you afraid of?

MARSDEN

[*Thinking in a panic*]
She sneaked into my soul to spy! . . .
[*Then boldly*]
Well then, a little truth for once in a way! . . .
[*Timidly*]

I'm afraid of—of life, Nina.

NINA

[*Nodding slowly*]

I know.
[*After a pause—queerly*]

The mistake began when God was created in a male image. Of course, women would see Him that way, but men should have been gentlemen enough, remembering their mothers, to make God a woman! But the God of Gods—the Boss—has always been a man. That makes life so perverted, and death so unnatural. We should have imagined life as created in the birth-pain of God the Mother. Then we would understand why we, Her children, have inherited pain, for we would know that our life's rhythm beats from Her great heart, torn with the agony of love and birth. And we would feel that death meant reunion with Her, a passing back into Her substance, blood of Her blood again, peace of Her peace!

[MARSDEN *has been listening to her fascinatedly. She gives a strange little laugh*]

Now wouldn't that be more logical and satisfying than having God a male whose chest thunders with egotism and is too hard for tired heads and thoroughly comfortless? Wouldn't it, Charlie?

MARSDEN

[*With a strange passionate eagerness*]
Yes! It would, indeed! It would, Nina!

NINA

[*Suddenly jumping to her feet and going to him—with a horrible moaning desolation*]
Oh, God, Charlie, I want to believe in something! I want to believe so I can feel! I want to feel that he is dead—my father! And I can't feel anything, Charlie! I can't feel anything at all!

[*She throws herself on her knees beside him and hides her face in her hands on his knees and begins to sob— stifled torn sounds*]

MARSDEN

[*Bends down, pats her head with trembling hands, soothes her with uncertain trembling words*]
There—there—don't—Nina, please—don't cry—you'll make yourself sick—come now—get up—do!

[*His hands grasping her arms he half raises her to her feet, but, her face still hidden in her hands, sobbing, she slips on to his lap like a little girl and hides her face on his shoulder. His expression becomes transported with a great happiness*]
[*In an ecstatic whisper*]
As I dreamed . . . with a deeper sweetness! . . .
[*He kisses her hair with a great reverence*]

There . . . this is all my desire . . . I am this kind
of lover . . . this is my love . . . she is my girl . . .
not woman . . . my little girl . . . and I am brave because of her little girl's pure love . . . and I am proud
. . . no more afraid . . . no more ashamed of being
pure! . . .
[*He kisses her hair again tenderly and smiles at himself*]
[*Then soothingly with a teasing incongruous gaiety*]
This will never do, Nina Cara Nina—never, never do, you
know—I can't permit it!

NINA

[*In a muffled voice, her sobbing beginning to ebb away
into sighs—in a young girl's voice*]
Oh, Charlie, you're so kind and comforting! I've wanted
you so!

MARSDEN

[*Immediately disturbed*]
Wanted? . . . wanted? . . . not that kind of wanted
. . . can she mean? . . .
[*Questioning hesitatingly*]
You've wanted me, Nina?

NINA

Yes,—awfully! I've been so homesick. I've wanted to run
home and 'fess up, tell how bad I've been, and be punished!
Oh, I've got to be punished, Charlie, out of mercy for me,
so I can forgive myself! And now Father dead, there's only
you. You will, won't you—or tell me how to punish myself?
You've simply got to, if you love me!

MARSDEN

[*Thinking intensely*]

If I love her! . . . oh, I do love her! . . .
[*Eagerly*]
Anything you wish, Nina—anything!

NINA

[*With a comforted smile, closing her eyes and cuddling
up against him*]
I knew you would. Dear old Charlie!
[*As he gives a wincing start*]
What is it?
[*She looks up into his face*]

MARSDEN

[*Forcing a smile—ironically*]
Twinge—rheumatics—getting old, Nina.
[*Thinking with wild agony*]
Dear old Charlie! . . . descended again into hell! . . .
[*Then in a flat voice*]
What do you want to be punished for, Nina?

NINA

[*In a strange, far-away tone, looking up not at him but
at the ceiling*]
For playing the silly slut, Charlie. For giving my cool
clean body to men with hot hands and greedy eyes which
they called love! Ugh!
[*A shiver runs over her body*]

MARSDEN

[*Thinking with sudden agony*]
Then she did! . . . the little filth! . . .

[*In his flat voice*]
You mean you—
[*Then pleadingly*]
But not—Darrell?

NINA

[*With simple surprise*]
Ned? No, how could I? The war hadn't maimed him.
There would have been no point in that. But I did with
others—oh, four or five or six or seven men, Charlie. I
forget—and it doesn't matter. They were all the same.
Count them all as one, and that one a ghost of nothing.
That is, to me. They were important to themselves, if I
remember rightly. But I forget.

MARSDEN

[*Thinking in agony*]
But why? . . . the dirty little trollop! . . . why? . . .
[*In his flat voice*]
Why did you do this, Nina?

NINA

[*With a sad little laugh*]
God knows, Charlie! Perhaps I knew at the time but I've
forgotten. It's all mixed up. There was a desire to be
kind. But it's horribly hard to give anything, and frightful
to receive! And to give love—oneself—not in this world!
And men are difficult to please, Charlie. I seemed to feel
Gordon standing against a wall with eyes bandaged and
these men were a firing squad whose eyes were also bandaged
—and only I could see! No, I was the blindest! I would

not see! I knew it was a stupid, morbid business, that I
was more maimed than they were, really, that the war
had blown my heart and insides out! And I knew too that
I was torturing these tortured men, morbidly super-sensitive
already, that they loathed the cruel mockery of my gift!
Yet I kept on, from one to one, like a stupid, driven animal
until one night not long ago I had a dream of Gordon
diving down out of the sky in flames and he looked at me
with such sad burning eyes, and all my poor maimed men,
too, seemed staring out of his eyes with a burning pain, and
I woke up crying, my own eyes burning. Then I saw what
a fool I'd been—a guilty fool! So be kind and punish me!

MARSDEN

[*Thinking with bitter confusion*]
I wish she hadn't told me this . . . it has upset me terribly! . . . I positively must run home at once . . .
Mother is waiting up . . . oh, how I'd love to hate this
little whore! . . . then I could punish! . . . I wish her
father were alive . . . "now he's dead there's only you,"
she said . . . "I've wanted you," . . .
[*With intense bitterness*]
Dear old Father Charlie now! . . . ha! . . . that's how
she wants me! . . .
[*Then suddenly in a matter-of-fact tone that is mockingly
like her father's*]
Then, under the circumstances, having weighed the pros and
cons, so to speak, I should say that decidedly the most
desirable course—

NINA

[*Drowsily—her eyes shut*]
You sound so like Father, Charlie.

MARSDEN

[*In the tone like her father's*]

—is for you to marry that young Evans. He is a splendid chap, clean and boyish, with real stuff in him, too, to make a career for himself if he finds a helpmeet who will inspire him to his best efforts and bring his latent ability to the surface.

NINA

[*Drowsily*]

Sam is a nice boy. Yes, it would be a career for me to bring a career to his surface. I would be busy—surface life—no more depths, please God! But I don't love him, Father.

MARSDEN

[*Blandly—in the tone like her father's*]

But you like him, Nina. And he loves you devotedly. And it's time you were having children—and when children come, love comes, you know.

NINA

[*Drowsily*]

I want children. I must become a mother so I can give myself. I am sick of sickness.

MARSDEN

[*Briskly*]

Then it's all settled?

NINA

[*Drowsily*]

Yes.

[*Very sleepily*]

Thank you, Father. You've been so kind. You've let me off too easily. I don't feel as if you'd punished me hardly at all. But I'll never, never do it again, I promise—never, never!—

[*She falls asleep and gives a soft little snore*]

MARSDEN

[*Still in her father's tones—very paternally—looking down*]

She's had a hard day of it, poor child! I'll carry her up to her room.

[*He rises to his feet with Nina sleeping peacefully in his arms. At this moment* SAM EVANS *enters from the right with the package of medicine in his hand*]

EVANS

[*Grinning respectfully*]

Here's the—

[*As he sees Nina*]

Oh!

[*Then excitedly*]

Did she faint?

MARSDEN

[*Smiling kindly at* EVANS—*still in her father's tones*]

Sssh! She's asleep. She cried and then she fell asleep— like a little girl.

[*Then benignantly*] .

But first we spoke a word about you, Evans, and I'm sure you have every reason to hope.

EVANS

[*Overcome, his eyes on his shuffling feet and twiddling cap*]

Thanks—I—I really don't know how to thank—

MARSDEN

[*Going to door—in his own voice now*]

I've got to go home. My mother is waiting up for me. I'll just carry Nina upstairs and put her on her bed and throw something over her.

EVANS

Can't I help you, Mr. Marsden?

MARSDEN

[*Dully*]

No.   I cannot help myself.

[*As* EVANS *looks puzzled and startled he adds with an ironical, self-mocking geniality*]

You'd better call me just Charlie after this.

[*He smiles bitterly to himself as he goes out*]

EVANS

[*Looks after him for a moment—then cannot restrain a joyful, coltish caper—gleefully*]

Good egg! Good old Charlie!

[*As if he had heard or guessed,* MARSDEN's *bitter laugh comes back from the end of the hallway*]

CURTAIN

ACT THREE

ACT THREE

SCENE: *Seven months or so later—the dining room of the*
EVANS' homestead in northern New York state—about
nine o'clock in the morning of a day in late spring of
the following year.

The room is one of those big, misproportioned dining
rooms that are found in the large, jigsaw country
houses scattered around the country as a result of the
rural taste for grandeur in the eighties. There is a
cumbersome hanging lamp suspended from chains over
the exact center of the ugly table with its set of straight-
backed chairs set back at spaced intervals against
the walls. The wall paper, a repulsive brown, is stained
at the ceiling line with damp blotches of mildew, and
here and there has started to peel back where the
strips join. The floor is carpeted in a smeary brown
with a dark red design blurred into it. In the left
wall is one window with starched white curtains look-
ing out on a covered side porch, so that no sunlight
ever gets to this room and the light from the window,
although it is a beautiful warm day in the flower garden
beyond the porch, is cheerless and sickly. There is a
door in the rear, to left of center, that leads to a hall
opening on the same porch. To the right of door a
heavy sideboard, a part of the set, displaying some
"company" china and glassware. In the right wall,
a door leading to the kitchen.

Nina is seated at the foot of the table, her back to the window, writing a letter. Her whole personality seems changed, her face has a contented expression, there is an inner calm about her. And her personal appearance has changed in kind, her face and figure have filled out, she is prettier in a conventional way and less striking and unusual; nothing remains of the strange fascination of her face except her unchangeably mysterious eyes.

NINA

[Reading what she has just written over to herself]
It's a queer house, Ned.   There is something wrong with its psyche, I'm sure.   Therefore you'd simply adore it. It's a hideous old place, a faded gingerbread with orange fixin's and numerous lightning rods.   Around it are acres and acres of apple trees in full bloom, all white and pinkish and beautiful, like brides just tripping out of church with the bridegroom, Spring, by the arm.
Which reminds me, Ned, that it's over six months since Sam and I were married and we haven't seen hide nor hair of you since the ceremony.   Do you think that is any nice way to act?   You might at least drop me a line. But I'm only joking.   I know how busy you must be now that you've got the chance you've always wanted to do research work.   Did you get our joint letter of congratulation written after we read of your appointment?
But to get back to this house.   I feel it has lost its soul and grown resigned to doing without it.   It isn't haunted by anything at all—and ghosts of some sort are the only normal life a house has—like our minds, you know.   So although last evening when we got here at first I said "obviously haunted" to myself, now that I've spent one night in it I know that whatever spooks there may once

have been have packed up their manifestations a long
time ago and drifted away over the grass, wisps of mist
between the apple trees, without one backward glance
of regret or recollection. It's incredible to think Sam
was born and spent his childhood here. I'm glad he
doesn't show it! We slept last night in the room he was
born in. Or rather he slept, I couldn't. I lay awake and
found it difficult to breathe, as if all the life in the air
had long since been exhausted in keeping the dying living a little longer. It was hard to believe anyone had
ever been born alive there. I know you're saying crossly
"She's still morbid" but I'm not. I've never been more
normal. I feel contented and placid.

[*Looking up from the letter, thinking embarrassedly*]
Should I have told him? . . . no . . . my own secret
. . . tell no one . . . not even Sam . . . why haven't I
told Sam? . . . it'd do him so much good . . . he'd feel
so proud of himself, poor dear . . . no . . . I want to
keep it just my baby . . . only mine . . . as long as I
can . . . and it will be time enough to let Ned know
when I go to New York . . . he can suggest a good
obstetrician . . . how delighted he'll be when he
hears! . . . he always said it would be the best thing for
me . . . well, I do feel happy when I think . . . and I
love Sam now . . . in a way . . . it will be his baby
too . . .

[*Then with a happy sigh, turns back to letter*]
But speaking of Sam's birth, you really must meet his
mother sometime. It's amazing how little she is like him,
a strange woman from the bit I saw of her last night.
She has been writing Sam regularly once a week ever
since she's known we were married, the must urgent invita-
tions to visit her. They were really more like commands,
or prayers. I suspect she is terribly lonely all by herself
in this big house. Sam's feeling toward her puzzles me.

I don't believe he ever mentioned her until her letters
began coming or that he'd ever have come to see the
poor woman if I hadn't insisted.   His attitude rather
shocked me.   It was just as though he'd forgotten he had
a mother.   And yet as soon as he saw her he was sweet
enough.   She seemed dreadfully upset to see Charlie with
us, until we'd explained it was thanks to his kindness and
in his car we were taking this deferred honeymoon.
Charlie's like a fussy old woman about his car, he's
afraid to let Sam or me drive it—

MARSDEN

[*Enters from the rear.   He is spruce, dressed immaculately, his face a bit tired and resigned, but smiling
kindly.   He has a letter in his hand*]
Good morning.
[*She gives a start and instinctively covers the letter with
her hand*]

NINA

Good morning.
[*Thinking amusedly*]
If he knew what I'd just written . . . poor old
Charlie! . . .
[*Then indicating the letter he carries*]
I see you're an early correspondent, too.

MARSDEN

[*With sudden jealous suspicion*]
Why did she cover it up like that? . . . whom is she
writing to? . . .

[*Coming toward her*]

Just a line to Mother to let her know we've not all been murdered by rum-bandits. You know how she worries.

NINA

[*Thinking with a trace of pitying contempt*]
Apron strings . . . still his devotion to her is touching . . . I hope if mine is a boy he will love me as much . . . oh, I hope it is a boy . . . healthy and strong and beautiful . . . like Gordon! . . .
[*Then suddenly sensing* MARSDEN's *curiosity—perfunctorily*]

I'm writing to Ned Darrell. I've owed him one for ages.
[*She folds it up and puts it aside*]

MARSDEN

[*Thinking glumly*]
I thought she'd forgotten him . . . still I suppose it's just friendly . . . and it's none of my business now she's married. . . .
[*Perfunctorily*]

How did you sleep?

NINA

Not a wink. I had the strangest feeling.

MARSDEN

Sleeping in a strange bed, I suppose.
[*Jokingly*]

Did you see any ghosts?

NINA

[*With a sad smile*]
No, I got the feeling the ghosts had all deserted the house

and left it without a soul—as the dead so often leave the
living—

[*She forces a little laugh*]

if you get what I mean.

MARSDEN

[*Thinking worriedly*]

Slipping back into that morbid tone . . . first time in a
long while . . .

[*Teasingly*]

Hello! Do I hear graveyards yawning from their sleep—
and yet I observe it's a gorgeous morning without, the
flowers are flowering, the trees are treeing with one another,
and you, if I mistake not, are on your honeymoon!

NINA

[*Immediately gaily mocking*]

Oh, very well, old thing! "God's in his heaven, all's right
with the world!" And Pippa's cured of the pip!

[*She dances up to him*]

MARSDEN

[*Gallantly*]

Pippa is certainly a pippin this morning!

NINA

[*Kisses him quickly*]

You deserve one for that! All I meant was that ghosts remind me of men's smart crack about women, you can't live
with them and can't live without them.

[*Stands still and looks at him teasingly*]

But there you stand proving me a liar by every breath you

draw! You're ghostless and womanless—and as sleek and satisfied as a pet seal!

> [*She sticks out her tongue at him and makes a face of superior scorn*]

Bah! That for you, 'Fraid-cat Charlie, you slacker bachelor!

> [*She runs to the kitchen door*]

I'm going to bum some more coffee! How about you?

MARSDEN

> [*With a forced smile*]

No, thank you.

> [*She disappears into the kitchen*]
>
> [*Thinking with bitter pain*]
>
> Ghostless! . . . if she only knew . . . that joking tone hides her real contempt! . . .
>
> [*Self-mockingly*]
>
> "But when the girls began to play 'Fraid-cat Charlie ran away!"
>
> [*Then rallying himself*]
>
> Bosh! . . . I haven't had such thoughts . . . not since their marriage . . . happy in her happiness . . . but is she happy? . . . in the first few months she was obviously playing a part . . . kissed him too much . . . as if she'd determined to make herself a loving wife . . . and then all of a sudden she became contented . . . her face filled out . . . her eyes lazily examined peace . . . pregnant . . . yes, she must be . . . I hope so. . . . why? . . . for her sake . . . my own, too . . . when she has a child I know I can entirely accept . . . forget I have lost her . . . lost her? . . . silly ass! . . . how can you lose what you never possessed? . . . except in dreams! . . .
>
> [*Shaking his head exasperatedly*]

Round and round . . . thoughts . . . damn pests! . . .
mosquitoes of the soul . . . whine, sting, suck one's
blood . . . why did I invite Nina and Sam on this tour
. . . it's a business trip with me, really . . , I need a
new setting for my next novel . . . "Mr. Marsden departs a bit from his familiar field" . . . well, there they
were stuck in the Professor's house . . . couldn't afford
a vacation . . . never had a honeymoon . . . I've pre-
tended to be done up every night so they could . . . I've
gone to bed right after dinner so they could be alone and
. . . I wonder if she can really like him . . . that
way? . . .

[*The sound of* EVANS' *voice and his mother's is heard
from the garden.* MARSDEN *goes over and carefully
peers out*]

Sam with his mother . . . peculiar woman . . . strong
. . . good character for a novel . . . no, she's too somber . . . her eyes are the saddest . . . and, at the same
time, the grimmest . . . they're coming in . . . I'll drive
around the country a bit . . . give them a chance for a
family conference . . . discuss Nina's pregnancy, I suppose . . . does Sam know? . . . he gives no indica-
tion . . . why do wives hide it from their husbands? . . .
ancient shame . . . guilty of continuing life, of bringing
fresh pain into the world . . .

[*He goes out, rear. The outside door in the hall is
heard being opened and* EVANS *and his mother evidently
meet* MARSDEN *as he is about to go out. Their voices, his
voice explaining, are heard, then the outer door being
opened and shut again as* MARSDEN *departs. A moment
later* EVANS *and his mother enter the dining room.* SAM
*looks timorously happy, as if he could not quite believe
in his good fortune and had constantly to reassure himself about it, yet he is riding the crest of the wave, he
radiates love and devotion and boyish adoration. He is*

a charming-looking fresh boy now. He wears a sweater and linen knickers, collegiate to the last degree. His mother is a tiny woman with a frail figure, her head and face, framed in iron-gray hair, seeming much too large for her body, so that at first glance she gives one the impression of a wonderfully made, lifelike doll. She is only about forty-five but she looks at least sixty. Her face with its delicate features must have once been of a romantic, tender, clinging-vine beauty, but what has happened to her has compressed its defenseless curves into planes, its mouth into the thin line around a locked door, its gentle chin has been forced out aggressively by a long reliance on clenched teeth. She is very pale. Her big dark eyes are grim with the prisoner-pain of a walled-in soul. Yet a sweet loving-kindness, the ghost of an old faith and trust in life's goodness, hovers girlishly, fleetingly, about the corners of her mouth and softens into deep sorrow the shadowy grimness of her eyes. Her voice jumps startlingly in tone from a caressing gentleness to a blunted flat assertiveness, as if what she said then was merely a voice on its own without human emotion to inspire it]

EVANS

[As they come in—rattling on in the cocksure boastful way of a boy showing off his prowess before his mother, confident of thrilled adulation]

In a few years you won't have to worry one way or another about the darned old apple crop. I'll be able to take care of you then. Wait and see! Of course, I'm not making so much now. I couldn't expect to. I've only just started. But I'm making good, all right, all right—since I got married—and it's only a question of time when— Why, to show you, Cole—he's the manager and the best egg ever—called me into his office and told me he'd had his eye on me, that my stuff was exactly what they wanted, and he thought I had the makings of a real find.

[*Proudly*]

How's that? That's certainly fair enough, isn't it?

MRS. EVANS

[*Vaguely—she has evidently not heard much of what he said*]

That's fine, Sammy.

[*Thinking apprehensively*]

I do hope I'm wrong! . . . but that old shiver of dread took me the minute she stepped in the door! . . . I don't think she's told Sammy but I got to make sure. . . .

EVANS

[*Seeing her preoccupation now—deeply hurt—testily*]

I'll bet you didn't hear a word I said! Are you still worrying about how the darn old apples are going to turn out?

MRS. EVANS

[*With a guilty start—protestingly*]

Yes, I did hear you, Sammy—every word! That's just what I was thinking about—how proud I am you're doing so wonderful well!

EVANS

[*Mollified but still grumbling*]

You'd never guess it from the gloomy way you looked!

[*But encouraged to go on*]

And Cole asked me if I was married—seemed to take a real personal interest—said he was glad to hear it because marriage was what put the right kind of ambition into a fellow—

unselfish ambition—working for his wife and not just himself—

[*Then embarrassedly*]
He even asked me if we were expecting an addition to the
family.

MRS. EVANS

[*Seeing this is her chance—quickly—forcing a smile*]
I've been meaning to ask you that myself, Sammy.
[*Blurts out apprehensively*]
She—Nina—she isn't going to have a baby, is she?

EVANS

[*With an indefinable guilty air—as if he were reluctant
to admit it*]
I—why—you mean, is she now? I don't think so, Mother.
[*He strolls over to the window whistling with an exag-
geratedly casual air, and looks out*]

MRS. EVANS

[*Thinking with grim relief*]
He don't know . . . there's that much to be thankful for,
anyway. . . .

EVANS

[*Thinking with intense longing*]
If that'd only happen! . . . soon! . . . Nina's begun to
love me . . . a little . . . I've felt it the last two
months . . . God, it's made me happy! . . . before that
she didn't . . . only liked me . . . that was all I asked
. . . never dared hope she'd come to love me . . . even
a little . . . so soon . . . sometimes I feel it's too good
to be true . . . don't deserve it . . . and now . . . if

that'd happen . . . then I'd feel sure . . . it'd be
there . . . half Nina, half me . . . living proof! . . .
[*Then an apprehensive note creeping in*]
And I know she wants a baby so much . . . one reason
why she married me . . . and I know she's felt right
along that then she'd love me . . . really love me . . .
[*Gloomily*]
I wonder why . . . ought to have happened before
this . . . hope it's nothing wrong . . . with me! . . .
[*He starts, flinging off this thought—then suddenly
clutching at a straw, turns hopefully to his mother*]
Why did you ask me that, Mother? D'you think—?

MRS. EVANS

[*Hastily*]
No, indeed! I don't think she is! I wouldn't say so at all!

EVANS

[*Dejectedly*]
Oh—I thought perhaps—
[*Then changing the subject*]
I suppose I ought to go up and say hello to Aunt Bessie.

MRS. EVANS

[*Her face becoming defensive—in blunted tones, a trifle
pleadingly*]
I wouldn't, Sammy. She hasn't seen you since you were
eight. She wouldn't know you. And you're on your honeymoon, and old age is always sad to young folks. Be happy
while you can!
[*Then pushing him toward door*]
Look here! You catch that friend, he's just getting his car
out. You drive to town with him, give me a chance to get to

know my daughter-in-law, and call her to account for how she's taking care of you!

[*She laughs forcedly*]

EVANS

[*Bursting out passionately*]
Better than I deserve! She's an angel, Mother! I know you'll love her!

MRS. EVANS

[*Gently*]
I do already, Sammy! She's so pretty and sweet!

EVANS

[*Kisses her—joyously*]
I'll tell her that. I'm going out this way and kiss her good-bye.

[*He runs out through the kitchen door*]

MRS. EVANS

[*Looking after him—passionately*]
He loves her! . . . he's happy! . . . that's all that counts! . . . being happy! . . .
[*Thinking apprehensively*]
If only she isn't going to have a baby . . . if only she doesn't care so much about having one . . . I got to have it out with her . . . got to! . . . no other way . . . in mercy . . . in justice . . . this has got to end with my boy . . . and he's got to live happy! . . .
[*At the sound of steps from the kitchen she straightens up in her chair stiffly*]

NINA

[*Comes in from the kitchen, a cup of coffee in her hand, smiling happily*]

Good morning—

[*She hesitates—then shyly*]

Mother.

[*She comes over and kisses her—slips down and sits on the floor beside. her*]

MRS. EVANS

[*Flusteredly—hurriedly*]

Good morning! It's a real fine day, isn't it? I ought to have been here and got your breakfast, but I was out gallivanting round the place with Sammy. I hope you found everything you wanted.

NINA

Indeed I did! And I ate so much I'm ashamed of myself!

[*She nods at the cup of coffee and laughs*]

See. I'm still at it.

MRS. EVANS

Good for you!

NINA

I ought to apologize for coming down so late. Sam should have called me. But I wasn't able to get to sleep until after daylight somehow.

MRS. EVANS

[*Strangely*]

You couldn't sleep? Why? Did you feel anything funny— about this house?

NINA

[*Struck by her tone—looks up*]

No. Why?

[*Thinking*]

How her face changes! . . . what sad eyes! . . .

MRS. EVANS

[*Thinking in an agony of apprehension*]

Got to start in to tell her . . . got to . . .

NINA

[*Apprehensive herself now*]

That sick dead feeling . . . when something is going to
happen . . . I felt it before I got the cable about Gordon . . .

[*Then taking a sip of coffee, and trying to be pleasantly
casual*]

Sam said you wanted to talk to me.

MRS. EVANS

[*Dully*]

Yes. You love my boy, don't you?

NINA

[*Startled—forcing a smile, quickly*]

Why, of course!

[*Reassuring herself*]

No, it isn't a lie . . . I do love him . . . the father of
my baby . . .

MRS. EVANS

[*Blurts out*]

Are you going to have a baby, Nina?

NINA

[*She presses* MRS. EVANS' *hand*]
[*Simply*]
Yes, Mother.

MRS. EVANS

[*In her blunt flat tones—with a mechanical rapidity to
her words*]
Don't you think it's too soon?   Don't you think you better
wait until Sammy's making more money? Don't you think it'll
be a drag on him and you?   Why don't you just go on being
happy together, just you two?

NINA

[*Thinking frightenedly*]
What is behind what she's saying? . . . that feeling of
death again! . . .
[*Moving away from her—repulsed*]
No, I don't think any of those things, Mrs. Evans.   I want
a baby—beyond everything!   We both do!

MRS. EVANS

[*Hopelessly*]
I know.
[*Then grimly*]
But you can't!   You've got to make up your mind you
can't!
[*Thinking fiercely—even with satisfaction*]
Tell her! . . . make her suffer what I was made to
suffer! . . . I've been too lonely! . . .

NINA

[*Thinking with terrified foreboding*]
I knew it! . . . Out of a blue sky . . . black! . . .
[*Springing to her feet—bewilderedly*]
What do you mean? How can you say a thing like that?

MRS. EVANS

[*Reaching out her hand tenderly, trying to touch Nina*]
It's because I want Sammy—and you, too, child—to be
happy.
[*Then as Nina shrinks away from her hand—in her
blunted tones*]
You just can't.

NINA

[*Defiantly*]
But I can! I have already! I mean—I am, didn't you
understand me?

MRS. EVANS

[*Gently*]
I know it's hard.
[*Then inexorably*]
But you can't go on!

NINA

[*Violently*]
I don't believe you know what you're saying! It's too terrible for you—Sam's own mother—how would you have felt
if someone—when you were going to have Sam—came to
you and said—?

MRS. EVANS

[*Thinking fiercely*]

Now's my chance! . . .

[*Tonelessly*]

They did say it! Sam's own father did—my husband! And
I said it to myself! And I did all I could, all my husband
could think of, so's I wouldn't—but we didn't know enough.
And right to the time the pains come on, I prayed Sammy'd
be born dead, and Sammy's father prayed, but Sammy was
born healthy and smiling, and we just had to love him, and
live in fear. He doubled the torment of fear we lived in.
And that's what you'd be in for. And Sammy, he'd go the
way his father went. And your baby, you'd be bringing it
into torment.

[*A bit violently*]

I tell you it'd be a crime—a crime worse than murder!

[*Then recovering—commiseratingly*]

So you just can't, Nina!

NINA

[*Who has been listening distractedly—thinking*]

Don't listen to her! . . . feeling of death! . . .what is
it? . . . she's trying to kill my baby! . . . oh, I hate
her! . . .

[*Hysterically resentful*]

What do you mean? Why don't you speak plainly?

[*Violently*]

I think you're horrible! Praying your baby would be born
dead! That's a lie! You couldn't!

MRS. EVANS

[*Thinking*]

I know what she's doing now . . . just what I did . . . trying not to believe . . .

[*Fiercely*]

But I'll make her! . . . she's got to suffer, too! . . . I been too lonely! . . . she's got to share and help me save my Sammy! . . .

[*With an even more blunted flat relentless tonelessness*]

I thought I was plain, but I'll be plainer. Only remember it's a family secret, and now you're one of the family. It's the curse on the Evanses. My husband's mother—she was an only child—died in an asylum and her father before her. I know that for a fact. And my husband's sister, Sammy's aunt, she's out of her mind. She lives on the top floor of this house, hasn't been out of her room in years, I've taken care of her. She just sits, doesn't say a word, but she's happy, she laughs to herself a lot, she hasn't a care in the world. But I remember when she was all right, she was always unhappy, she never got married, most people around here were afraid of the Evanses in spite of their being rich for hereabouts. They knew about the craziness going back, I guess, for heaven knows how long. I didn't know about the Evanses until after I'd married my husband. He came to the town I lived in, no one there knew about the Evanses. He didn't tell me until after we were married. He asked me to forgive him, he said he loved me so much he'd have gone mad without me, said I was his only hope of salvation. So I forgave him. I loved him an awful lot. I said to myself, I'll be his salvation—and maybe I could have been if we hadn't had Sammy born. My husband kept real well up to then. We'd swore we'd never have children, we never forgot to be careful for two whole years. Then one night we'd both gone to a dance, we'd both had a little punch to drink, just enough—to forget—driving home in the moonlight—that moonlight!—such little things at the back of big things!

NINA

[*In a dull moan*]
I don't believe you! I won't believe you!

MRS. EVANS

[*Drones on*]
My husband, Sammy's father, in spite of all he and I fought against it, he finally gave in to it when Sammy was only eight, he couldn't keep up any more living in fear for Sammy, thinking any minute the curse might get him, every time he was sick, or had a headache, or bumped his head, or started crying, or had a nightmare and screamed, or said something queer like children do naturally.

[*A bit stridently*]
Living like that with that fear is awful torment! I know that! I went through it by his side! It nearly drove me crazy, too—but I didn't have it in my blood! And that's why I'm telling you! You got to see you can't, Nina!

NINA

[*Suddenly breaking out—frenziedly*]
I don't believe you! I don't believe Sam would ever have married me if he knew—!

MRS. EVANS

[*Sharply*]

Who said Sammy knew? He don't know a single thing about it! That's been the work of my life, keeping him from knowing. When his father gave up and went off into it I sent Sammy right off to boarding school. I told him his father was sick, and a little while after I sent word his father was dead, and from then on until his father did really die during Sammy's second year to college, I kept him away at school in winter and camp in summers and I went to see him, I never let him come home.

[*With a sigh*]

It was hard, giving up Sammy, knowing I was making him forget he had a mother. I was glad taking care of them two kept me so busy I didn't get much chance to think then. But here's what I've come to think since, Nina: I'm certain sure my husband might have kept his mind with the help of my love if I hadn't had Sammy. And if I'd never had Sammy I'd never have loved Sammy—or missed him, would I?—and I'd have kept my husband.

NINA

[*Not heeding this last—with wild mockery*]

And I thought Sam was so normal—so healthy and sane —not like me! I thought he'd give me such healthy, happy children and I'd forget myself in them and learn to love him!

MRS. EVANS

[*Horrified, jumping to her feet*]

Learn to? You told me you did love Sammy!

NINA

No! Maybe I almost have—lately—but only when I thought
of his baby! Now I hate him!

> [*She begins to weep hysterically.* MRS. EVANS *goes to
> her and puts her arms around her.* NINA *sobs out*]

Don't touch me! I hate you, too! Why didn't you tell him
he must never marry!

MRS. EVANS

What reason could I give, without telling him everything?
And I never heard about you till after you were married.
Then I wanted to write to you but I was scared he might
read it. And I couldn't leave her upstairs to come away
to see you. I kept writing Sammy to bring you here right
off, although having him come frightened me to death for
fear he might get to suspect something. You got to get
him right away from here, Nina! I just kept hoping you
wouldn't want children right away—young folks don't nowa-
days—until I'd seen you and told you everything. And I
thought you'd love him like I did his father, and be satisfied
with him alone.

NINA

> [*Lifting her head—wildly*]

No! I don't! I won't! I'll leave him!

MRS. EVANS

> [*Shaking her, fiercely*]

You can't! He'd go crazy sure then! You'd be a devil!
Don't you see how he loves you?

NINA

[*Breaking away from her—harshly*]

Well, I don't love him! I only married him because he needed me—and I needed children! And now you tell me I've got to kill my—·oh, yes, I see I've got to, you needn't argue any more! I love it too much to make it run that chance! And I hate it too, now, because it's sick, it's not my baby, it's his!

[*With terrible ironic bitterness*]

And still you can dare to tell me I can't even leave Sam!

MRS. EVANS

[*Very sadly and bitterly*]

You just said you married him because he needed you. Don't he need you now—more'n ever? But I can't tell you not to leave him, not if you don't love him. But you oughtn't to have married him when you didn't love him. And it'll be your fault, what'll happen.

NINA

[*Torturedly*]

What will happen?—what do you mean?—Sam will be all right—just as he was before—and it's not my fault anyway! —it's not my fault!

[*Then thinking conscience-strickenly*]

Poor Sam . . . she's right . . . it's not his fault . . . it's mine . . . I wanted to use him to save myself . . . I acted the coward again . . . as I did with Gordon . . .

MRS. EVANS

[*Grimly*]

You know what'll happen to him if you leave him—after all I've told you!

[*Then breaking into intense pleading*]

Oh, I'd get down on my knees to you, don't make my boy
run that risk! You got to give one Evans, the last one,
a chance to live in this world! And you'll learn to love him,
if you give up enough for him!

[*Then with a grim smile*]

Why, I even love that idiot upstairs, I've taken care of her
so many years, lived her life for her with my life, you might
say. You give your life to Sammy, then you'll love him
same as you love yourself. You'll have to! That's sure
as death!

[*She laughs a queer gentle laugh full of amused bitterness*]

NINA

[*With a sort of dull stupid wonderment*]

And you've found peace?—

MRS. EVANS

[*Sardonically*]

There's peace in the green fields of Eden, they say! You got
to die to find out!

[*Then proudly*]

But I can say I feel proud of having lived fair to them that
gave me love and trusted in me!

NINA

[*Struck—confusedly*]

Yes—that's true, isn't it?

[*Thinking strangely*]

Lived fair . . . pride . . . trust . . . play the game!
. . . who is speaking to me . . . Gordon! . . . oh, Gor-

don, do you mean I must give Sam the life I didn't give
you? . . . Sam loved you too . . . he said, if we have a
boy, we'll call him Gordon in Gordon's honor . . . Gordon's honor! . . . what must I do now in your honor,
Gordon? . . . yes! . . . I know! . . .

[*Speaking mechanically in a dull voice*]

All right, Mother. I'll stay with Sam. There's nothing
else I can do, is there, when it isn't his fault, poor boy!

[*Then suddenly snapping and bursting out in a despairing cry*]

But I'll be so lonely! I'll have lost my baby!

[*She sinks down on her knees at* MRS. EVANS' *feet—
piteously*]

Oh, Mother, how can I keep on living?

MRS. EVANS

[*Thinking miserably*]

Now she knows my suffering . . . now I got to help her
. . . she's got a right to have a baby . . . another
baby . . . sometime . . . somehow . . . she's giving her
life to save my Sammy . . . I got to save her! . . .

[*Stammeringly*]

Maybe, Nina—

NINA

[*Dully and resentfully again now*]

And how about Sam? You want him to be happy, don't
you? It's just as important for him as it is for me that I
should have a baby! If you know anything at all about
him, you ought to see that!

MRS. EVANS

[*Sadly*]

I know that. I see that in him, Nina.

[*Gropingly*]

There must be a way—somehow. I remember when I was
carrying Sam, sometimes I'd forget I was a wife, I'd only
remember the child in me. And then I used to wish I'd gone
out deliberate in our first year, without my husband knowing, and picked a man, a healthy male to breed by, same's
we do with stock, to give the man I loved a healthy child.
And if I didn't love that other man nor him me where would
be the harm? Then God would whisper: "It'd be a sin, adultery, the worst sin!" But after He'd gone I'd argue back
again to myself, then we'd have a healthy child, I needn't
be afraid! And maybe my husband would feel without ever
knowing how he felt it, that I wasn't afraid and that child
wasn't cursed and so he needn't fear and I could save him.

[*Then scornfully*]

But I was too afraid of God then to have ever done it!

[*Then very simply*]

He loved children so, my poor husband did, and the way
they took to him, you never saw anything like it, he was a
natural born father. And Sammy's the same.

NINA

[*As from a distance—strangely*]

Yes, Sammy's the same. But I'm not the same as you.

[*Defiantly*]

I don't believe in God the Father!

MRS. EVANS

[*Strangely*]

Then it'd be easy for you.

[*With a grim smile*]

And I don't believe in Him, neither, not any more. I used to be a great one for worrying about what's God and what's devil, but I got richly over it living here with poor folks that was being punished for no sins of their own, and me being punished with them for no sin but loving much.

[*With decision*]

Being happy, that's the nearest we can ever come to knowing what's good! Being happy, that's good! The rest is just talk!

[*She pauses—then with a strange austere sternness*]

I love my boy, Sammy. I could see how much he wants you to have a baby. Sammy's got to feel sure you love him— to be happy. Whatever you can do to make him happy is good—is good, Nina! I don't care what! You've got to have a healthy baby—sometime—so's you can both be happy! It's your rightful duty!

NINA

[*Confusedly—in a half-whisper*]

Yes, Mother.

[*Thinking longingly*]

I want to be happy! . . . it's my right . . . and my duty! . . .

[*Then suddenly in guilty agony*]

Oh, my baby . . . my poor baby . . . I'm forgetting you . . . desiring another after you are dead! . . . I feel you beating against my heart for mercy . . . oh! . . .

[*She weeps with bitter anguish*]

MRS. EVANS

[*Gently and with deep sympathy*]

I know what you're suffering. And I wouldn't say what I

just said now only I know us two mustn't see each other
ever again. You and Sammy have got to forget me.

> [*As* NINA *makes a motion of protest—grimly and in-
> exorably*]

Oh, yes, you will—easy. People forget everything. They
got to, poor people! And I'm saying what I said about a
healthy baby so's you will remember it when you need to,
after you've forgotten—this one.

NINA

> [*Sobbing pitifully*]

Don't! Please, Mother!

MRS. EVANS

> [*With sudden tenderness—gathering* NINA *up in her
> arms, brokenly*]

You poor child! You're like the daughter of my sorrow!
You're closer to me now than ever Sammy could be! I want
you to be happy!

> [*She begins to sob, too, kissing* NINA'S *bowed head*]

CURTAIN

ACT FOUR

ACT FOUR

SCENE: *An evening early in the following winter about seven months later. The* PROFESSOR'S *study again. The books in the cases have never been touched, their austere array shows no gaps, but the glass separating them from the world is gray with dust, giving them a blurred ghostly quality. The table, although it is the same, is no longer the* PROFESSOR'S *table, just as the other furniture in the room, by its disarrangement, betrays that the* PROFESSOR'S *well-ordered mind no longer trims it to his personality. The table has become neurotic. Volumes of the Encyclopedia Britannica mixed up with popular treatises on Mind Training for Success, etc., looking startlingly modern and disturbing against the background of classics in the original, are slapped helter-skelter on top of each other on it. The titles of these books face in all directions, no one volume is placed with any relation to the one beneath it—the effect is that they have no connected meaning. The rest of the table is littered with an ink bottle, pens, pencils, erasers, a box of typewriting paper, and a typewriter at the center before the chair, which is pushed back, setting the rug askew. On the floor beside the table are an overflowing wastepaper basket, a few sheets of paper and the rubber cover for the typewriter like a collapsed tent. The rocking chair is no longer at center but has been pulled nearer the table, directly faces it*

119

*with its back to the bench. This bench in turn has been
drawn much closer, but is now placed more to the rear
and half-faces front, its back squarely to the door in
the corner.*

EVANS *is seated in the* PROFESSOR'S *old chair. He has
evidently been typing, or is about to type, for a sheet of
paper can be seen in the machine. He smokes a pipe,
which he is always relighting whether it needs it or not,
and which he bites and shifts about and pulls in and out
and puffs at nervously. His expression is dispirited,
his eyes shift about, his shoulders are collapsed submissively. He seems much thinner, his face drawn and
sallow. The collegiate clothes are no longer natty,
they need pressing and look too big for him.*

EVANS

[*Turns to his typewriter and pounds out a few words
with a sort of aimless desperation—then tears the sheet
out of the machine with an exclamation of disgust,
crumples it up and throws it violently on the floor, pushing his chair back and jumping to his feet*]

Hell!

[*He begins pacing up and down the room, puffing at his
pipe, thinking tormentedly*]

No use . . . can't think of a darn thing . . . well, who
could dope out a novel ad on another powdered milk, anyway? . . . all the stuff been used already . . . Tartars
conquering on dried mare's milk . . . Metchnikoff, emi-
nent scientist . . been done to death . . . but simply
got to work out som 'hing or . . . Cole said, what's been
the matter with you lately? . . . you started off so well

. . . I thought you were a real find, but your work's
fallen off to nothing . . .

[*He sits down on the edge of the bench nearby, his shoulders hunched—despondently*]

Couldn't deny it . . . been going stale ever since we
came back from that trip home . . . no ideas . . . I'll
get fired . . . sterile . . .

[*With a guilty terror*]

in more ways than one, I guess! . . .

[*He springs to his feet as if this idea were a pin stuck in
him—lighting his already lighted pipe, walks up and
down again, forcing his thoughts into other channels*]

Bet the old man turns over in his grave at my writing ads
in his study . . . maybe that's why I can't . . . bum
influence . . . try tomorrow in my bedroom . . . sleeping alone . . . since Nina got sick . . . some woman's
sickness . . . wouldn't tell me . . . too modest . . .
still, there are some things a husband has a right to know
. . . especially when we haven't . . . in five months . . .
doctor told her she mustn't, she said . . . what doctor?
. . . she's never said . . . what the hell's the matter with
you, do you think Nina's lying? . . . no . . . but . . .

[*Desperately*]

If I was only sure it was because she's really sick . . .
not just sick of me! . . .

[*He sinks down in the rocking chair despondently*]

Certainly been a big change in her . . . since that visit
home . . . what happened between Mother and her? . . .
she says nothing . . . they seemed to like each other
. . . both of them cried when we left . . . still, Nina insisted on going that same day and Mother seemed anxious
to get rid of us . . . can't make it out . . . next few
weeks Nina couldn't be loving enough . . . I never was
so happy . . . then she crashed . . . strain of waiting
and hoping she'd get pregnant . . . and nothing hap-

pening . . . that's what did it . . . my fault! . . . how
d'you know? . . . you can't tell that! . . .

[*He jumps to his feet again—walks up and down again
distractedly*]

God, if we'd only have a kid! . . . then I'd show them
all what I could do! . . . Cole always used to say I had
the stuff, and Ned certainly thought so. . . .

[*With sudden relieved excitement*]

By gosh, I was forgetting! . . . Ned's coming out tonight . . . forgot to tell Nina . . . mustn't let her get
wise I got him to come to look her over . . . she'd hate
me for swallowing my pride after he's never been to see
us . . . but I had to . . . this has got my goat . . . I've
got to know what's wrong . . . and Ned's the only one I
can trust . . .

[*He flings himself on chair in front of desk and, picking
up a fresh sheet of paper, jams it into the machine*]

Gosh, I ought to try and get a new start on this before
it's time . . .

[*He types a sentence or two, a strained frown of con-
centration on his face. NINA comes silently through the
door and stands just inside it looking at him. She has
grown thin again, her face is pale and drawn, her movements are those of extreme nervous tension*]

NINA

[*Before she can stifle her immediate reaction of contempt
and dislike*]

How weak he is! . . . he'll never do anything . . .
never give me my desire . . . if he'd only fall in love
with someone else . . . go away . . . not be here in my
father's room . . . I even have to give him a home . . .
if he'd disappear . . . leave me free . . . if he'd die
. . .

[*Checking herself—remorsefully*]
I must stop such thoughts . . . I don't mean it . . .
poor Sam! . . . trying so hard . . . loving me so much
. . . I give so little in return . . . he feels I'm always
watching him with scorn . . . I can't tell him it's with
pity . . . how can I help watching him? . . . help
worrying over his worry because of what it might lead to
. . . after what his mother . . . how horrible life is!
. . . he's worried now . . . he doesn't sleep . . . I hear
him tossing about . . . I must sleep with him again soon
. . . he's only home two nights a week . . . it isn't fair
of me . . . I must try . . . I must! . . . he suspects
my revulsion . . . it's hurting him . . . oh, poor dead
baby I dared not bear, how I might have loved your
father for your sake! . . .

EVANS

[*Suddenly feeling her presence, jerks himself to his
feet—with a diffident guilty air which is noticeable about
him now whenever he is in her presence*]
Hello, dear. I thought you were lying down.
[*Guiltily*]
Did the noise of my typing bother you? I'm terribly sorry!

NINA

[*Irritated in spite of herself*]
Why is he always cringing? . . .
[*She comes forward to the chair at center and sits
down—forcing a smile*]
But there's nothing to be terribly sorry about!
[*As he stands awkward and confused, like a schoolboy
who has been called on to recite and cannot and is being
"bawled out" before the class, she forces a playful tone*]
Goodness, Sam, how tragic you can get about nothing at all!

EVANS

[*Still forced to justify himself—contritely*]

I know it isn't pleasant for you having me drag my work
out here, trying to pound out rotten ads.

[*With a short laugh*]

Trying to is right!

[*Blurts out*]

I wouldn't do it except that Cole gave me a warning to buck
up—or get out.

NINA

[*Stares at him, more annoyed, her eyes hardening, thinking*]

Yes! . . . he'll always be losing one job, getting another,
starting with a burst of confidence each time, then . . .

[*Cutting him with a careless sneering tone*]

Well, it isn't a job to worry much about losing, is it?

EVANS

[*Wincing pitiably*]

No, not much money. But I used to think there was a fine
chance to rise there—but of course that's my fault, I haven't
made good—

[*He finishes miserably*]

somehow.

NINA

[*Her antagonism giving way to remorseful pity*]

What makes me so cruel? . . . he's so defenseless . . .
his mother's baby . . . poor sick baby! . . . poor Sam!
. . .

[*She jumps to her feet and goes over to him*]

EVANS

[*As she comes—with a defensive, boastful bravery*]
Oh, I can get another job just as good, all right—maybe a
lot better.

NINA

[*Reassuringly*]
Certainly, you can! And I'm sure you're not going to lose
this one. You're always anticipating trouble.

[*She kisses him and sits on the arm of his chair, putting
an arm around his neck and pulling his head on to her
breast*]
And it isn't your fault, you big goose, you! It's mine. I
know how hard it makes everything for you, being tied to a
wife who's too sick to be a wife. You ought to have married a big strapping, motherly—

EVANS

[*In the seventh heaven now—passionately*]
Bunk! All the other women in the world aren't worth your
little finger! It's you who ought to have married someone
worth while, not a poor fish like me! But no one could love
you more than I do, no matter what he was!

NINA

[*Presses his head on her breast, avoiding his eyes, kisses
him on the forehead*]
And I love you, Sam.
[*Staring out over his head—with loving pity, thinking*]
I almost do . . . poor unfortunate boy! . . . at these
moments . . . as his mother loves him . . . but that

isn't enough for him . . . I can hear his mother saying, "Sammy's got to feel sure you love him . . . to be happy." . . . I must try to make him feel sure . . .

[*Speaking gently*]

I want you to be happy, Sam.

EVANS

[*His face transformed with happiness*]

I am—a hundred times more than I deserve!

NINA

[*Presses his head down on her breast so he cannot see her eyes—gently*]

Ssshh.

[*Thinking sadly*]

I promised her . . . but I couldn't see how hard it would be to let him love me . . . after his baby . . . was gone . . . it was hard even to keep on living . . . after that operation . . . Gordon's spirit followed me from room to room . . . poor reproachful ghost! . . .

[*With bitter mockery*]

Oh, Gordon, I'm afraid this is a deeper point of honor than any that was ever shot down in flames! . . . what would your honor say now? . . . "Stick to him! . . . play the game!" . . . oh, yes, I know . . . I'm sticking . . . but he isn't happy . . . I'm trying to play the game . . . then why do I keep myself from him? . . . but I was really sick . . . for a time after . . . since then, I couldn't . . . but . . . oh, I'll try . . . I'll try soon . . .

[*Tenderly—but having to force herself to say it*]

Doesn't my boy want to sleep with me again—sometime soon?

EVANS

[Passionately—hardly able to believe his ears]
Oh, it'd be wonderful, Nina! But are you sure you really
want me to—that you'll feel well enough?

NINA

[Repeats his words as if she were memorizing a lesson]
Yes, I want you to. Yes, I'll feel well enough.
*[He seizes her hand and kisses it in a passionately grate-
ful silence]*
[She thinks with resigned finality]
There, Sammy's mother and Gordon . . . I'll play the
game . . . it will make him happy for a while . . . as
he was in those weeks after we'd left his mother . . .
when I gave myself with a mad pleasure in torturing
myself for his pleasure! . . .
[Then with weary hopelessness]
He'll be happy until he begins to feel guilty again because
I'm not pregnant . . .
[With a grim bitter smile]
Poor Sam, if he only knew the precautions . . . as if I
wouldn't die rather than take the slightest chance of
that happening! . . . ever again . . . what a tragic joke
it was on both of us! . . . I wanted my baby so! . . .
oh, God! . . . his mother said . . . "You've got to have
a healthy baby . . . sometime . . . it's your rightful
duty". . . that seemed right then . . . but now . . . it
seems cowardly . . . to betray poor Sam . . . and vile to
give myself . . . without love or desire . . . and yet
I've given myself to men before without a thought, just
to give them a moment's happiness . . . can't I do that
again? . . . when it's a case of Sam's happiness? . . .
and my own? . . .

[*She gets up from beside him with a hunted movement*]
It must be half past eight. Charlie's coming to bring his
suggestions on my outline for Gordon's biography.

EVANS

[*His bliss shattered—dejectedly*]
Always happens . . . just as we get close . . . some-
thing comes between . . .
[*Then confusedly*]
Say, I forgot to tell you Ned's coming out tonight.

NINA

[*Astonished*]
Ned Darrell?

EVANS

Sure. I happened to run into him the other day and invited
him and he said Saturday evening. He couldn't tell what
train. Said never mind meeting him.

NINA

[*Excitedly*]
Why didn't you tell me before, you big booby!
[*She kisses him*]
There, don't mind. But it's just like you. Now someone'll
have to go down to the store. And I'll have to get the spare
room ready.
[*She hurries to the doorway. He follows her*]

EVANS

I'll help you.

NINA

You'll do nothing of the kind! You'll stay right down-

stairs and bring them in here and cover up my absence.
Thank heavens, Charlie won't stay long if Ned is here.

[*The doorbell rings—excitedly*]

There's one of them now. I'll run upstairs. Come up and
tell me if it's Ned—and get rid of Charlie.

[*She kisses him playfully and hurries out*]

EVANS

[*Looking after her—thinks*]

She seems better tonight . . . happier . . . she seems
to love me . . . if she'll only get all well again, then
everything will . . .

[*The bell rings again*]

I must give Ned a good chance to talk to her . . .

[*He goes out to the outer door—returns a moment later
with* MARSDEN. *The latter's manner is preoccupied and
nervous. His face has an expression of anxiety which
he tries to conceal. He seems a prey to some inner fear
he is trying to hide even from himself and is resolutely
warding off from his consciousness. His tall, thin body
stoops as if a part of its sustaining will had been removed*]

EVANS

[*With a rather forced welcoming note*]

Come on in, Charlie. Nina's upstairs lying down.

MARSDEN

[*With marked relief*]

Then by all means don't disturb her. I just dropped in to
bring back her outline with the suggestions I've made.

[*He has taken some papers out of his pocket and hands
them to* EVANS]

I couldn't have stayed but a minute in any event. Mother
is a bit under the weather these days.

EVANS

[*Perfunctorily*]

Too bad.

[*Thinking vindictively*]

Serve her right, the old scandal-monger, after the way she's gossiped about Nina! . . .

MARSDEN

[*With assumed carelessness*]

Just a little indigestion.   Nothing serious but it annoys her terribly.

[*Thinking frightenedly*]

That dull pain she complains of . . . I don't like it . . . and she won't see anyone but old Doctor Tibbetts . . . she's sixty-eight . . . I can't help fearing . . . no! . . .

EVANS

[*Bored—vaguely*]

Well, I suppose you've got to be careful of every little thing when you get to her age.

MARSDEN

[*Positively bristling*]

Her age?   Mother isn't so old!

EVANS

[*Surprised*]

Over sixty-five, isn't she?

MARSDEN

[*Indignantly*]

You're quite out there!   She's still under sixty-five—and in health and spirits she isn't more than fifty!   Everyone remarks that!

[*Annoyed at himself*]

Why did I lie to him about her age? . . . I must be on edge . . . Mother is rather difficult to live with these days, getting me worried to death, when it's probably nothing . . .

EVANS

[*Annoyed in his turn—thinking*]

Why all the fuss? . . . as if I gave a damn if the old girl was a million! . . .

[*Indicating the papers*]

I'll give these to Nina first thing in the morning.

MARSDEN

[*Mechanically*]

Righto. Thank you.

[*He starts to go toward door—then turns—fussily*]

But you'd better take a look while I'm here and see if it's clear. I've written on the margins. See if there's anything you can't make out.

[EVANS *nods helplessly and begins reading the sheets, going back beneath the lamp*]

MARSDEN

[*Looking around him with squeamish disapproval*]

What a mess they've made of this study . . . poor Professor! . . . dead and forgotten . . . and his tomb desecrated . . . does Sam write his ads here of a week-end now? . . . the last touch! . . . and Nina labors with love at Gordon's biography . . . whom the Professor hated! . . . "life is so full of a number of things!" . . . why does everyone in the world think they can write?

. . . but I've only myself to blame . . . why in the devil
did I ever suggest it to her? . . . because I hoped my
helping her while Sam was in the city would bring us
alone together? . . . but I made the suggestion before
she had that abortion performed! . . . how do you know
she did? . . . because I know! . . . there are psychic
affinities . . . her body confessed . . . and since then,
I've felt an aversion . . . as if she were a criminal . . .
she is! . . . how could she? . . . why? . . . I thought
she wanted a child . . . but evidently I don't know her
. . . I suppose, afraid it would spoil her figure . . . her
flesh . . . her power to enslave men's senses . . . mine
. . . and I had hoped . . . looked forward to her becoming a mother . . . for my peace of mind. . . .

[*Catching himself—violently*]

Shut up! . . . what a base creature I'm becoming! . . .
to have such thoughts when Mother is sick and I ought
to be thinking only of her! . . . and it's none of my damn
business, anyway! . . .

[*Glaring at* EVANS *resentfully as if he were to blame*]

Look at him! . . . he'll never suspect anything! . . .
what a simple-simon! . . . he adored Gordon as a news-
boy does a champion pugilist! . . . and Nina writes of
Gordon as if he had been a demi-god! . . . when actually
he came from the commonest people! . . .

[*He suddenly speaks to* EVANS *with a really savage satisfaction*]

Did I tell you I once looked up Gordon's family in Beach-
ampton? A truly deplorable lot! When I remembered
Gordon and looked at his father I had either to suspect a
lover in the wood pile or to believe in an Immaculate Con-
ception . . . that is, until I saw his mother! Then a stork
became the only conceivable explanation!

EVANS

[*Who has only half-heard and hasn't understood, says vaguely*]

I never saw his folks.

[*Indicating the papers*]

I can make this all out all right.

MARSDEN

[*Sarcastically*]

I'm glad it's understandable!

EVANS

[*Blunderingly*]

I'll give it to Nina—and I hope your mother is feeling better tomorrow.

MARSDEN

[*Piqued*]

Oh, I'm going. Why didn't you tell me if I was interrupting —your writing!

EVANS

[*Immediately guilty*]

Oh, come on, Charlie, don't get peevish, you know I didn't mean—

[*The bell rings. Evans stammers in confusion, trying at a nonchalant air*]

Hello! That must be Ned. You remember Darrell. He's coming out for a little visit. Excuse me.

[*He blunders out of the door*]

MARSDEN

[*Looking after him with anger mixed with alarmed suspicion and surprise*]

Darrell? . . . what's he doing here? . . . have they been
meeting? . . . perhaps he was the one who performed
the . . . no, his idea was she ought to have a child
. . . but if she came and begged him? . . . but why
should Nina beg not to have a baby? . . .

[*Distractedly*]

Oh, I don't know! . . . it's all a sordid mess! . . . I
ought to be going home! . . . I don't want to see
Darrell! . . .

[*He starts for the door—then struck by a sudden thought,
stops*]

Wait . . . I could ask him about Mother . . . yes . . .
good idea . . .

[*He comes back to the middle of the room, front, and is
standing there when* DARRELL *enters, followed by* EVANS.
DARRELL *has not changed in appearance except that his
expression is graver and more thoughtful. His manner
is more convincingly authoritative, more mature. He
takes in* MARSDEN *from head to foot with one compre-
hensive glance*]

EVANS

[*Awkwardly*]

Ned, you remember Charlie Marsden?

MARSDEN

[*Holding out his hand, urbanely polite*]

How are you, Doctor?

DARRELL

[*Shaking his hand—briefly*]

Hello.

EVANS

I'll go up and tell Nina you're here, Ned.

[*He goes, casting a resentful glance at* MARSDEN]

MARSDEN

[*Awkwardly, as* DARRELL *sits down in the chair at center, goes over and stands by the table*]

I was on the point of leaving when you rang. Then I decided to stop and renew our acquaintance.

[*He stoops and picks up one sheet of paper, and puts it back carefully on the table*]

DARRELL

[*Watching him—thinking*]

Neat . . . suspiciously neat . . . he's an old maid who seduces himself in his novels . . . so I suspect . . . I'd like a chance to study him more closely. . . .

MARSDEN

[*Thinking resentfully*]

What a boor! . . . he might say something! . . .

[*Forcing a smile*]

And I wanted to ask a favor of you, a word of advice as to the best specialist, the very best, it would be possible to consult—

DARRELL

[*Sharply*]

On what?

MARSDEN

[*Almost naïvely*]

My mother has a pain in her stomach.

DARRELL

[*Amused—dryly*]
Possibly she eats too much.

MARSDEN

[*As he bends and carefully picks another sheet from the
floor to place it as carefully on the table*]
She doesn't eat enough to keep a canary alive. It's a dull,
constant pain, she says. She's terribly worried. She's terrified by the idea of cancer. But, of course, that's perfect
rot, she's never been sick a day in her life and—

DARRELL

[*Sharply*]
She's showing more intelligence about her pain than you
are.

MARSDEN

[*Bending down for another sheet, his voice trembling
with terror*]
I don't understand—quite. Do you mean to say you
think—?

DARRELL

[*Brutally*]
It's possible.
[*He has pulled out his pen and a card and is writing*]
[*Thinking grimly*]
Explode a bomb under him, as I did once before . . .
only way to get him started doing anything. . . .

MARSDEN

[*Angrily*]
But—that's nonsense!

DARRELL

[*With satisfaction—unruffledly*]
People who are afraid to face unpleasant possibilities until
it's too late commit more murders and suicides than—
[*Holds out card*]
Doctor Schultz is your man. Take her to see him—
tomorrow!

MARSDEN

[*Bursting out in anger and misery*]
Damn it, you're condemning her without—!
[*He breaks down chokingly*]
You've no damn right!—
[*He bends down, trembling all over, to pick up another
piece of paper*]

DARRELL

[*Genuinely astonished and contrite*]
And I thought he was so ingrown he didn't care a damn
about anyone! . . . his mother . . . now I begin to see
him . . .
[*He jumps from his chair and going to* MARSDEN *puts a
hand on his shoulder—kindly*]
I beg your pardon, Marsden. I only wanted to drive it in
that all delay is dangerous. Your mother's pain may be
due to any number of harmless causes, but you owe it to her
to make sure. Here.
[*He hands out the card*]

MARSDEN

[*Straightens up and takes it, his eyes grateful now—
humbly*]
Thank you. I'll take her to see him tomorrow.
[EVANS *comes in*]

EVANS

[*To* MARSDEN, *blunderingly*]

Say, Charlie, I don't want to hurry you but Nina wants some things at the store before it closes, and if you'd give me a lift—

MARSDEN

[*Dully*]

Of course.   Come along.

[*He shakes hands with* DARRELL]

Good night, Doctor—and thank you.

DARRELL

Good night.

[MARSDEN *goes, followed by* EVANS]

EVANS

[*Turns in the doorway and says meaningly*]

Nina'll be right down.   For Pete's sake, have a good heart-to-heart talk with her, Ned!

DARRELL

[*Frowning—impatiently*]

Oh—all right!   Run along.

[EVANS *goes*]

[DARRELL *remains standing near the table looking after them, thinking about* MARSDEN]

Queer fellow, Marsden . . . mother's boy still . . . if she dies what will he do? . . .

[*Then dismissing* MARSDEN *with a shrug of his shoulders*]

Oh, well, he can always escape life in a new book. . . .

[*He moves around the table examining its disorder critically, then sits down in armchair—amused*]

Evidences of authorship . . . Sam's ads? . . . isn't making good, he said . . . was I wrong in thinking he had stuff in him? . . . hope not . . . always liked Sam, don't know why exactly . . . said Nina'd gotten into a bad state again . . . what's happened to their marriage? . . . I felt a bit sorry for myself at their wedding . . . not that I'd ever fallen . . . but I did envy him in a way . . . she always had strong physical attraction for me . . . that time I kissed her . . . one reason I've steered clear since . . . take no chances on emotional didos . . . need all my mind on my work . . . got rid of even that slight suspicion . . . I'd forgotten all about her . . . she's a strange girl . . . interesting case . . . I should have kept in touch on that account . . . hope she'll tell me about herself . . . can't understand her not having child . . . it's so obviously the sensible thing . . .
[Cynically]
Probably why . . . to expect common sense of people proves you're lacking in it yourself! . . .

NINA

[Enters silently. She has fixed herself up, put on her best dress, arranged her hair, rouged, etc.—but it is principally her mood that has changed her, making her appear a younger, prettier person for the moment. DARRELL immediately senses her presence, and, looking up, gets to his feet with a smile of affectionate admiration. She comes quickly over to him saying with frank pleasure]
Hello, Ned. I'm certainly glad to see you again—after all these years!

DARRELL

[As they shake hands—smiling]
Not as long as all that, is it?

[*Thinking admiringly*]
Wonderful-looking as ever . . . Sam is a lucky
devil! . . .

NINA

[*Thinking*]
Strong hands like Gordon's . . . take hold of you . . .
not like Sam's . . . yielding fingers that let you fall
back into yourself . . .
[*Teasingly*]
I ought to cut you dead after the shameful way you've ig-
nored us!

DARRELL

[*A bit embarrassedly*]
I've really meant to write.
[*His eyes examining her keenly*]
Been through a lot since I saw her . . . face shows it
. . . nervous tension pronounced . . . hiding behind her
smile . . .

NINA

[*Uneasy under his glance*]
I hate that professional look in his eyes . . . watching
symptoms . . . without seeing me . . .
[*With resentful mockery*]
Well, what do you suspect is wrong with the patient now,
Doctor?
[*She laughs nervously*]
Sit down, Ned. I suppose you can't help your diagnosing
stare.
[*She turns from him and sits down in the rocker at
center*]

DARRELL

[*Quickly averting his eyes—sits down—jokingly*]
Same old unjust accusation! You were always reading diag-

nosis into me, when what I was really thinking was what
fine eyes you had, or what a becoming gown, or—

NINA

[*Smiling*]
Or what a becoming alibi you could cook up! Oh, I know
you!
[*With a sudden change of mood she laughs gaily and*
naturally]
But you're forgiven—that is, if you can explain why you've
never been to see us.

DARRELL

Honestly, Nina, I've been so rushed with work I haven't
had a chance to go anywhere.

NINA

Or an inclination!

DARRELL

[*Smiling*]
Well—maybe.

NINA

Do you like the Institute so much?
[*He nods gravely*]
Is it the big opportunity you wanted?

DARRELL

[*Simply*]
I think it is.

NINA

[*With a smile*]
Well, you're the taking kind for whom opportunities are
made!

DARRELL

[*Smiling*]
I hope so.

NINA

[*Sighing*]
I wish that could be said of more of us—
[*Then quickly*]
—meaning myself.

DARRELL

[*Thinking with a certain satisfaction*]
Meaning Sam . . . that doesn't look hopeful for future
wedded bliss! . . .
[*Teasingly*]
But I heard you were "taking an opportunity" to go in for
literature—collaborating with Marsden.

NINA

No, Charlie is only going to advise.   He'd never deign to
appear as co-author.   And besides, he never appreciated the
real Gordon.   No one did except me.

DARRELL

[*Thinking caustically*]
Gordon myth strong as ever . . . root of her trouble
still . . .
[*Keenly inquisitive*]
Sam certainly appreciated him, didn't he?

NINA

[*Not remembering to hide her contempt*]
Sam?   Why, he's the exact opposite in every way!

DARRELL

[*Caustically thinking*]
These heroes die hard . . . but perhaps she can write
him out of her system. . . .
[*Persuasively*]
Well, you're going ahead with the biography, aren't you?
I think you ought to.

NINA

[*Dryly*]
For my soul, Doctor?
[*Listlessly*]
I suppose I will. I don't know. I haven't much time. The
duties of a wife—
[*Teasingly*]
By the way, if it isn't too rude to inquire, aren't you getting
yourself engaged to some fair lady or other?

DARRELL

[*Smiling—but emphatically*]
Not on your life! Not until after I'm thirty-five, at least!

NINA

[*Sarcastically*]
Then you don't believe in taking your own medicine? Why,
Doctor! Think of how much good it would do you!—
[*Excitedly with a hectic sarcasm*]
—if you had a nice girl to love—or was it learn to love?—
and take care of—whose character you could shape and
whose life you could guide and make what you pleased, in
whose unselfish devotion you could find peace!

[More and more bitterly sarcastic]
And you ought to have a baby, Doctor! You will never
know what life is, you'll never be really happy until you've
had a baby, Doctor—a fine, healthy baby!
[She laughs a bitter, sneering laugh]

DARRELL

[After a quick, keen glance, thinking]
Good! . . . she's going to tell . . .
[Meekly]
I recognize my arguments. Was I really wrong on every
point, Nina?

NINA

[Harshly]
On every single point, Doctor!

DARRELL

[Glancing at her keenly]
But how? You haven't given the baby end of it a chance yet,
have you?

NINA

[Bitterly]
Oh, haven't I?
[Then bursts out with intense bitterness]
I'll have you know I'm not destined to bear babies, Doctor!

DARRELL

[Startledly]
What's that? . . . why not? . . .
[Again with a certain satisfaction]
Can she mean Sam? . . . that he . .
[Soothingly—but plainly disturbed]

Why don't you begin at the beginning and tell me all about
it? I feel responsible.

NINA

[*Fiercely*]
You are!

[*Then wearily*]
And you're not. No one is. You didn't know. No one
could know.

DARRELL

[*In same tone*]
Know what?

[*Thinking with the same eagerness to believe something
he hopes*]
She must mean no one could know that Sam wasn't . . .
but I might have guessed it . . . from his general weakness . . . poor unlucky devil . . .

[*Then as she remains silent—urgingly*]
Tell me. I want to help you, Nina.

NINA

[*Touched*]
It's too late, Ned.

[*Then suddenly*]
I've just thought—Sam said he happened to run into you.
That isn't so, is it? He went to see you and told you how
worried he was about me and asked you out to see me,
didn't he?

[*As* DARRELL *nods*]
Oh, I don't mind! It's even rather touching.

[*Then mockingly*]
Well, since you're out here professionally, and my husband

wants me to consult you, I might as well give you the whole case history!

[*Wearily*]

I warn you it isn't pretty, Doctor! But then life doesn't seem to be pretty, does it? And, after all, you aided and abetted God the Father in making this mess. I hope it'll teach you not to be so cocksure in future.

[*More and more bitterly*]

I must say you proceeded very unscientifically, Doctor!

[*Then suddenly starts her story in a dull monotonous tone recalling that of* EVANS' *mother in the previous Act*]

When we went to visit Sam's mother I'd known for two months that I was going to have a baby.

DARRELL

[*Startled—unable to hide a trace of disappointment*]

Oh, then you actually were?

[*Thinking disappointedly and ashamed of himself for being disappointed*]

All wrong, what I thought . . . she was going to . . . then why didn't she? . . .

NINA

[*With a strange happy intensity*]

Oh, Ned, I loved it more than I've ever loved anything in my life—even Gordon! I loved it so it seemed at times that Gordon must be its real father, that Gordon must have come to me in a dream while I was lying asleep beside Sam! And I was happy! I almost loved Sam then! I felt he was a good husband!

DARRELL

[*Instantly repelled—thinking with scornful jealousy*] Ha! . . . the hero again! . . . comes to her bed! . . . puts horns on poor Sam! . . . becomes the father of his child! . . . I'll be damned if hers isn't the most idiotic obsession I ever . . .

NINA

[*Her voice suddenly becoming flat and lifeless*] And then Sam's mother told me I couldn't have my baby. You see, Doctor, Sam's great-grandfather was insane, and Sam's grandmother died in an asylum, and Sam's father had lost his mind for years before he died, and an aunt who is still alive is crazy. So of course I had to agree it would be wrong—and I had an operation.

DARRELL

[*Who has listened with amazed horror—profoundly shocked and stunned*] Good God! Are you crazy, Nina? I simply can't believe! It would be too hellish! Poor Sam, of all people! [*Bewilderedly*] Nina! Are you absolutely sure?

NINA

[*Immediately defensive and mocking*] Absolutely, Doctor! Why? Do you think it's I who am crazy? Sam looks so healthy and sane, doesn't he? He fooled you completely, didn't he? You thought he'd be an ideal husband for me! And poor Sam's fooling himself too because he doesn't know anything about all this—so you can't blame him, Doctor!

DARRELL

[*Thinking in a real panic of horror—and a flood of protective affection for her*]
God, this is too awful! . . . on top of all the rest! . . .
how did she ever stand it! . . . she'll lose her mind too!
. . . and it's my fault! . . . . . .
[*Getting up, comes to her and puts his hands on her shoulders, standing behind her—tenderly*]
Nina! I'm so damn sorry! There's only one possible thing
to do now. You'll have to make Sam give you a divorce.

NINA

[*Bitterly*]
Yes? Then what do you suppose would be his finish? No,
I've enough guilt in my memory now, thank you! I've got
to stick to Sam!
[*Then with a strange monotonous insistence*]
I've promised Sam's mother I'd make him happy! He's
unhappy now because he thinks he isn't able to give me a
child. And I'm unhappy because I've lost my child. So I
must have another baby—somehow—don't you think, Doctor?—to make us both happy?
[*She looks up at him pleadingly. For a moment they
stare into each other's eyes—then both turn away in
guilty confusion*]

DARRELL

[*Bewilderedly thinking*]
That look in her eyes . . . what does she want me
to think? . . . why does she talk so much about being
happy? . . . am I happy? . . . I don't know . . . what
is happiness? . . .

[*Confusedly*]

Nina, I don't know what to think.

NINA

[*Thinking strangely*]

That look in his eyes . . . what did he mean? . . .

[*With the same monotonous insistence*]

You must know what to think. I can't think it out myself any more. I need your advice—your *scientific* advice this time, if you please, Doctor. I've thought and thought about it. I've told myself it's what I ought to do. Sam's own mother urged me to do it. It's sensible and kind and just and good. I've told myself this a thousand times and yet I can't quite convince something in me that's afraid of something. I need the courage of someone who can stand outside and reason it out as if Sam and I were no more than guinea pigs. You've got to help me, Doctor! You've got to show me what's the sane—the truly sane, you understand!— thing I must do for Sam's sake, and my own.

DARRELL

[*Thinking confusedly*]

What do I have to do? . . . this was all my fault . . . I owe her something in return . . . I owe Sam something . . . I owe them happiness! . . .

[*Irritably*]

Damn it, there's a humming in my ears! . . . I've caught some fever . . . I swore to live coolly . . . let me see. . . .

[*In a cold, emotionless professional voice, his face like a mask of a doctor*]

A doctor must be in full possession of the facts, if he is to advise. What is it precisely that Sam's wife has thought so much of doing?

NINA

[In the same insistent tone]
Of picking out a healthy male about whom she cared nothing and having a child by him that Sam would believe was his child, whose life would give him confidence in his own living, who would be for him a living proof that his wife loved him.

[Confusedly, strangely and purposefully]
This doctor is healthy. . . .

DARRELL

[In his ultra-professional manner—like an automaton of a doctor]
I see. But this needs a lot of thinking over. It isn't easy to prescribe—

[Thinking]
I have a friend who has a wife . . . I was envious at his wedding . . . but what has that to do with it? . . . damn it, my mind won't work! . . . it keeps running away to her . . . it wants to mate with her mind . . . in the interest of Science? . . . what damned rot I'm thinking! . . .

NINA

[Thinking as before]
This doctor is nothing to me but a healthy male . . . when he was Ned he once kissed me . . . but I cared nothing about him . . . so that's all right, isn't it, Sam's Mother?

DARRELL

[*Thinking*]
Let me see. . . . I am in the laboratory and they are
guinea pigs . . . in fact, in the interest of science, I can
be for the purpose of this experiment, a healthy guinea pig
myself and still remain an observer . . . I observe my
pulse is high, for example, and that's obviously because I
am stricken with a recurrence of an old desire . . . desire
is a natural male reaction to the beauty of the female
. . . her husband is my friend. . . . I have always tried
to help him . . .
[*Coldly*]
I've been considering what Sam's wife told me and her rea-
soning is quite sound. The child can't be her husband's.

NINA

Then you agree with Sam's mother? She said: "Being happy
is the nearest we can ever come to knowing what good is!"

DARRELL

I agree with her decidedly. Sam's wife should find a healthy
father for Sam's child at once. It is her sane duty to her
husband.
[*Worriedly thinking*]
Have I ever been happy? . . . I have studied to cure
the body's unhappiness . . . I have watched happy
smiles form on the lips of the dying . . . I have experi-
enced pleasure with a number of women I desired but
never loved . . . I have known a bit of honor and a trifle
of self-satisfaction . . . this talk of happiness seems to
me extraneous . . .

NINA

[*Beginning to adopt a timid, diffident, guilty tone*]
This will have to be hidden from Sam so he can never know!
Oh, Doctor, Sam's wife is afraid!

DARRELL

[*Sharply professional*]
Nonsense! This is no time for timidity! Happiness hates
the timid! So does Science! Certainly Sam's wife must conceal her action! To let Sam know would be insanely cruel of
her—and stupid, for then no one could be the happier for
her act!

[*Anxiously thinking*]
Am I right to advise this? . . . yes, it is clearly the ra-
tional thing to do . . . but this advice betrays my friend!
. . . no, it saves him! . . . it saves his wife . . . and if
a third party should know a little happiness . . . is
he any poorer, am I any the less his friend because I
saved him? . . . no, my duty to him is plain . . . and
my duty as an experimental searcher after truth . . . to
observe these three guinea pigs, of which I am one . . .

NINA

[*Thinking determinedly*]
I must have my baby! . . .
[*Timidly—gets from her chair and half-turns toward
him—pleadingly*]
You must give his wife courage, Doctor. You must free
her from her feeling of guilt.

DARRELL

There can only be guilt when one deliberately neglects one's

manifest duty to life. Anything else is rot! This woman's
duty is to save her husband and herself by begetting a
healthy child!

> [*Thinking guiltily and instinctively moving away from
> her*]
> I am healthy . . . but he is my friend . . . there is
> such a thing as honor! . . .

NINA

> [*Determinedly*]
> I must take my happiness! . . .
> [*Frightenedly—comes after him*]

But she is ashamed. It's adultery. It's wrong.

DARRELL

> [*Moving away again—with a cold sneering laugh of im-
> patience*]

Wrong! Would she rather see her husband wind up in an
asylum? Would she rather face the prospect of going to
pot mentally, morally, physically herself through year after
year of devilling herself and him? Really, Madame, if you
can't throw overboard all such irrelevant moral ideas, I'll
have to give up this case here and now!

> [*Thinking frightenedly*]
> Who is talking? . . . is he suggesting me? . . . but you
> know very well I can't be the one, Doctor! . . . why
> not, you're healthy and it's a friendly act for all con-
> cerned . . .

NINA

> [*Thinking determinedly*]
> I must have my baby! . . .

[*Going further toward him—she can now touch him with her hand*]

Please, Doctor, you must give her strength to do this right thing that seems to her so right and then so wrong!

[*She puts out her hand and takes one of his*]

DARRELL

[*Thinking frightenedly*]

Whose hand is this? . . . it burns me . . . I kissed her once . . . her lips were cold . . . now they would burn with happiness for me! . . .

NINA

[*Taking his other hand and slowly pulling him around to face her, although he does not look at her—pleadingly*]

Now she feels your strength. It gives her the courage to ask you, Doctor, to suggest the father. She has changed, Doctor, since she became Sam's wife. She can't bear the thought now of giving herself to any man she could neither desire nor respect. So each time her thoughts come to the man she must select they are afraid to go on! She needs your courage to choose!

DARRELL

[*As if listening to himself*]

Sam is my friend . . . well, and isn't she your friend? . . . her two hands are so warm! . . . I must not even hint at my desire! . . .

[*Judicially calm*]

Well, the man must be someone who is not unattractive to her physically, of course.

NINA

Ned always attracted her.

DARRELL

[*Thinking frightenedly*]
What's that she said? . . . Ned? . . . attracts? . . .
[*In same tone*]
And the man should have a mind that can truly understand
—a scientific mind superior to the moral scruples that cause
so much human blundering and unhappiness.

NINA

She always thought Ned had a superior mind.

DARRELL

[*Thinking frightenedly*]
Did she say Ned? . . . she thinks Ned . . . ?
[*In same tone*]
The man should like and admire her, he should be her good
friend and want to help her, but he should not love her—
although he might, without harm to anyone, desire her.

NINA

Ned does not love her—but he used to like her and, I think,
desire her. Does he now, Doctor?

DARRELL

[*Thinking*]
Does he? . . . who is he? . . . he is Ned! . . . Ned is
I! . . . I desire her! . . . I desire happiness! . . .
[*Tremblingly now—gently*]
But, Madame, I must confess the Ned you are speaking of
is I, and I am Ned.

NINA

[*Gently*]

And I am Nina, who wants her baby.

> [*Then she reaches out and turns his head until his face faces hers but he keeps his eyes down—she bends her head meekly and submissively—softly*]

I should be so grateful, Ned.

> [*He starts, looks up at her wildly, makes a motion as though to take her in his arms, then remains fixed for a moment in that attitude, staring at her bowed head as she repeats submissively*]

I should be so humbly grateful.

DARRELL

> [*Suddenly falling on his knees and taking her hand in both of his and kissing it humbly—with a sob*]

Yes—yes, Nina—yes—for your happiness—in that spirit!

> [*Thinking—fiercely triumphant*]

I shall be happy for a while! . . .

NINA

> [*Raising her head—thinking—proudly triumphant*]

I shall be happy! . . . I shall make my husband happy! . . .

CURTAIN

ACT FIVE

ACT FIVE

SCENE: *The sitting room of a small house* EVANS *has rented in a seashore suburb near New York. It is a bright morning in the following April.*

The room is a typical sitting room of the quantity-production bungalow type. Windows on the left look out on a broad porch. A double doorway in rear leads into the hall. A door on right, to the dining room. NINA *has tried to take the curse of offensive, banal newness off the room with some of her own things from her old home but the attempt has been half-hearted in the face of such overpowering commonness, and the result is a room as disorganized in character as was the* PROFESSOR's *study in the last Act.*

The arrangement of the furniture follows the same pattern as in preceding scenes. There is a Morris chair and a round golden oak table at left of center, an upholstered chair, covered with bright chintz at center, a sofa covered with the same chintz at right.

NINA *is sitting in the chair at center. She has been trying to read a book but has let this drop listlessly on her lap. A great change is noticeable in her face and bearing. She is again the pregnant woman of Act Three but this time there is a triumphant strength about her expression, a ruthless self-confidence in her eyes. She has grown stouter, her face has filled out. One gets no*

159

impression of neurotic strain from her now, she seems
nerveless and deeply calm.

NINA

[*As if listening for something within her—joyfully*]
There! . . . that can't be my imagination . . . I felt it
plainly . . . life . . . my baby . . . my only baby . . .
the other never really lived . . . this is the child of
my love! . . . I love Ned! . . . I've loved him ever
since that first afternoon . . . when I went to him . . .
so scientifically! . . .
[*She laughs at herself*]
Oh, what a goose I was! . . . then love came to me . . .
in his arms . . . happiness! . . . I hid it from him . . .
I saw he was frightened . . . his own joy frightened him
. . . I could feel him fighting with himself . . . during all those afternoons . . . our wonderful afternoons
of happiness! . . . and I said nothing . . . I made myself be calculating . . . so when he finally said . . .
dreadfully disturbed . . . "Look here, Nina, we've done
all that is necessary, playing with fire is dangerous"
. . . I said, "You're quite right, Ned, of all things I
don't want to fall in love with you!" . . .
[*She laughs*]
He didn't like that! . . . he looked angry . . . and
afraid . . . then for weeks he never even phoned . . . I
waited . . . it was prudent to wait . . . but every day
I grew more terrified . . . then just as my will was
breaking, his broke . . . he suddenly appeared again
. . . but I held him to his aloof doctor's pose and sent
him away, proud of his will power . . . and sick of himself with desire for me! . . . every week since then he's
been coming out here . . . as my doctor . . . we've
talked about our child wisely, dispassionately . . . as if

it were Sam's child . . . we've never given in to our
desire . . . and I've watched love grow in him until I'm
sure . . .
[*With sudden alarm*]
But am I? . . . he's never once mentioned love . . .
perhaps I've been a fool to play the part. I've played
. . . it may have turned him against me . . .
[*Suddenly with calm confidence*]
No . . . he does . . . I feel it . . . it's only when I
start thinking, I begin to doubt . . .
[*She settles back and stares dreamily before her—a
pause*]
There . . . again . . . his child! . . . my child moving in my life . . . my life moving in my child . . . the
world is whole and perfect . . . all things are each
other's . . . life is . . . and the is is beyond reason
. . . questions die in the silence of this peace . . . I am
living a dream within the great dream of the tide . . .
breathing in the tide I dream and breathe back my dream
into the tide . . . suspended in the movement of the tide,
I feel life move in me, suspended in me . . . no whys
matter . . . there is no why . . . I am a mother . . .
God is a Mother . . .
[*She sighs happily, closing her eyes. A pause*]
[*Evans enters from the hallway in rear. He is dressed
carefully but his clothes are old ones—shabby collegiate
gentility—and he has forgotten to shave. His eyes look
pitiably harried, his manner has become a distressingly
obvious attempt to cover up a chronic state of nervous
panic and guilty conscience. He stops inside the doorway and looks at her with a pitiable furtiveness, arguing
with himself, trying to get up his courage*]
Tell her! . . . go on! . . . you made up your mind to,
didn't you? . . . don't quit now! . . . tell her you've
decided . . . for her sake . . . to face the truth . . . that

she can't love you . . . she's tried . . . she's acted like
a good sport . . . but she's beginning to hate you . . .
and you can't blame her . . . she wanted children
. . . and you haven't been able . . .
[*Protesting feebly*]
But I don't know for certain . . . that that's my
fault . . .
[*Then bitterly*]
Aw, don't kid yourself, if she'd married someone else . . .
if Gordon had lived and married her . . . I'll bet in the
first month she'd . . . you'd better resign from the whole
game . . . with a gun! . . .
[*He swallows hard as if he were choking back a sob—
then savagely*]
Stop whining! . . . go on and wake her up! . . . say
you're willing to give her a divorce so she can marry
some real guy who can give her what she ought to
have! . . .
[*Then with sudden terror*]
And if she says yes? . . . I couldn't bear it! . . . I'd
die without her! . . .
[*Then with a somber alien forcefulness*]
All right . . . good riddance! . . . I'd have the guts
to bump off then, all right! . . . that'd set her free . . .
come on now! . . . ask her! . . .
[*But his voice begins to tremble uncertainly again as he
calls*]

Nina.

NINA

[*Opens her eyes and gazes calmly, indifferently at him*]

Yes?

EVANS

[*Immediately terrified and beaten—thinking*]

I can't! . . . the way she looks at me! . . . she'd say yes! . . .

[*Stammering*]

I hate to wake you up but—it's about time for Ned to come, isn't it?

NINA

[*Calmly*]

I wasn't asleep.

[*Thinking as if she found it hard to concentrate on him, to realize his existence*]

This man is my husband . . . it's hard to remember that . . . people will say he's the father of my child. . . .

[*With revulsion*]

That's shameful! . . . and yet that's exactly what I wanted! . . . wanted! . . . not now! . . . now I love Ned! . . . I won't lose him! . . . Sam must give me a divorce . . . I've sacrificed enough of my life . . . what has he given me? . . . not even a home . . . I had to sell my father's home to get money so we could move near his job . . . and then he lost his job! . . . now he's depending on Ned to help him get another! . . . my love! . . . how shameless! . . .

[*Then contritely*]

Oh, I'm unjust . . . poor Sam doesn't know about Ned . . . and it was I who wanted to sell the place . . . I was lonely there . . . I wanted to be near Ned. . . .

EVANS

[*Thinking in agony*]

What's she thinking? . . . probably lucky for me I don't know! . . .

[*Forcing a brisk air as he turns away from her*]

I hope Ned brings that letter he promised me to the manager

of the Globe company. I'm keen to get on the job again.

NINA

[*With scornful pity*]

Oh, I guess Ned will bring the letter. I asked him not to
forget.

EVANS

I hope they'll have an opening right off. We can use the
money.

[*Hanging his head*]

I feel rotten, living on you when you've got so little.

NINA

[*Indifferently but with authority, like a governess to a
small boy*]

Now, now!

EVANS

[*Relieved*]

Well, it's true.

[*Then coming to her—humbly ingratiating*]

You've felt a lot better lately, haven't you, Nina?

NINA

[*With a start—sharply*]

Why?

EVANS

You look ever so much better. You're getting fat.

[*He forces a grin*]

NINA

[*Curtly*]

Don't be absurd, please! As a matter of fact, I don't feel a
bit better.

EVANS

[*Thinking despondently*]

Lately, she jumps on me every chance she gets . . . as if everything I did disgusted her! . . .

[*He strays over to the window and looks out listlessly*]

I thought we'd get some word from Charlie this morning saying if he was coming down or not. But I suppose he's still too broken up over his mother's death to write.

NINA

[*Indifferently*]

He'll probably come without bothering to write.

[*Vaguely—wonderingly*]

Charlie . . . dear old Charlie . . . I've forgotten him, too. . . .

EVANS

I think that's Ned's car now. Yes. It's stopping. I'll go out and meet him.

[*He starts for the door in rear*]

NINA

[*Sharply, before she can restrain the impulse*]

Don't be such a fool!

EVANS

[*Stops—stammers confusedly*]

What—what's the matter?

NINA

[*Controlling herself—but irritably*]

Don't mind me. I'm nervous.

[*Thinking guiltily*]

One minute I feel ashamed of him for making such a fool of himself over my lover . . . the next minute something hateful urges me to drive him into doing it! . . .

[*The maid has answered the ring and opened the outer door.* NED DARRELL *comes in from the rear. His face looks older. There is an expression of defensive bitterness and self-resentment about his mouth and eyes. This vanishes into one of desire and joy as he sees* NINA. *He starts toward her impulsively*]

Nina!

[*Then stops short as he sees* EVANS]

NINA

[*Forgetting* EVANS, *gets to her feet as if to receive* DARRELL *in her arms—with love*]

Ned!

EVANS

[*Affectionately and gratefully*]

Hello, Ned!

[*He holds out his hand which* DARRELL *takes mechanically*]

DARRELL

[*Trying to overcome his guilty embarrassment*]

Hello, Sam. Didn't see you.

[*Hurriedly reaching in his coat pocket*]

Before I forget, here's that letter. I had a talk over the phone with Appleby yesterday. He's pretty sure there's an opening—

[*With a condescension he can't help*]

—but you'll have to get your nose on the grindstone to make good with him.

EVANS

[*Flushing guiltily—forcing a confident tone*]

You bet I will!

[*Then gratefully and humbly*]

Gosh, Ned, I can't tell you how grateful I am!

DARRELL

[*Brusquely, to hide his embarrassment*]
Oh, shut up! I'm only too glad.

NINA

[*Watching* EVANS *with a contempt that is almost gloating —in a tone of curt dismissal*]
You'd better go and shave, hadn't you, if you're going to town?

EVANS

[*Guiltily, passing his hand over his face—forcing a brisk, purposeful air*]
Yes, of course. I forgot I hadn't. Excuse me, will you?
[*This to* DARRELL. EVANS *hurries out, rear*]

DARRELL

[*As soon as he is out of earshot—turning on* NINA *accusingly*]
How can you treat him that way? It makes me feel—like a swine!

NINA

[*Flushing guiltily—protestingly*]
What way?
[*Then inconsequentially*]
He's always forgetting to shave lately.

DARRELL

You know what I mean, Nina!
[*Turns away from her—thinking bitterly*]

What a rotten liar I've become! . . . and he trusts me absolutely! . . .

NINA

[*Thinking frightenedly*]
Why doesn't he take me in his arms? . . . oh, I feel he doesn't love me now! . . . he's so bitter! . . .
[*Trying to be matter-of-fact*]
I'm sorry, Ned. I don't mean to be cross but Sam does get on my nerves.

DARRELL

[*Thinking bitterly*]
Sometimes I almost hate her! . . . if it wasn't for her I'd have kept my peace of mind . . . no good for anything lately, damn it! . . . but it's idiotic to feel guilty . . . if Sam only didn't trust me! . . .
[*Then impatiently*]
Bosh! . . . sentimental nonsense! . . . end justifies means! . . . this will have a good end for Sam, I swear to that! . . . why doesn't she tell him she's pregnant? . . . what's she waiting for? . . .

NINA

[*Thinking passionately, looking at him*]
Oh, my lover, why don't you kiss me? . . .
[*Imploringly*]
Ned! Don't be cross with me, please!

DARRELL

[*Fighting to control himself—coldly*]
I'm not cross, Nina. Only you must admit these triangular scenes are, to say the least, humiliating.
[*Resentfully*]
I won't come out here again!

NINA

[*With a cry of pain*]

Ned!

DARRELL

[*Thinking exultingly at first*]
She loves me! . . . she's forgotten Gordon! . . . I'm
happy! . . . do I love her? . . . no! . . . I won't!
. . . I can't! . . . think what it would mean to
Sam! . . . to my career! . . . be objective about it! . . .
you guinea pig! . . . I'm her doctor . . . and Sam's
. . . I prescribed child for them . . . that's all there is
to it! . . .

NINA

[*Torn between hope and fear*]
What is he thinking? . . . he's fighting his love . . . oh,
my lover! . . .
[*Again with longing*]

Ned!

DARRELL

[*Putting on his best professional air, going to her*]
How do you feel today? You look as if you might have a
little fever.
[*He takes her hand as if to feel her pulse*]
[*Her hand closes over his. She looks up into his face.
He keeps his turned away*]

NINA

[*Straining up toward him—with intense longing—thinking*]
I love you! . . . take me! . . . what do I care for anything in the world but you! . . . let Sam die! . . .

DARRELL

[*Fighting himself—thinking*]

Christ! . . . touch of her skin! . . . her nakedness! . . . those afternoons in her arms! happiness! . . . what do I care for anything else? . . . to hell with Sam! . . .

NINA

[*Breaking out passionately*]

Ned! I love you! I can't hide it any more! I won't! I love you, Ned!

DARRELL

[*Suddenly taking her in his arms and kissing her frantically*]

Nina! Beautiful!

NINA

[*Triumphantly—between kisses*]

You love me, don't you? Say you do, Ned!

DARRELL

[*Passionately*]

Yes! Yes!

NINA

[*With a cry of triumph*]

Thank God! At last you've told me! You've confessed it to yourself! Oh, Ned, you've made me so happy!

[*There is a ring from the front door bell.* DARRELL *hears it. It acts like an electric shock on him. He tears himself away from her. Instinctively she gets up too and moves to the lounge at right*]

DARRELL

[*Stupidly*]

Someone—at the door.

[*He sinks down in the chair by the table at left*]
[*Thinking torturedly*]
I said I loved her! . . . she won! . . . she used my
desire! . . . but I don't love her! . . . I won't! . . .
she can't own my life! . . .
[*Violently—almost shouts at her*]
I don't, Nina! I tell you I don't!

NINA

[*The maid has just gone to the front door*]
Sshh!
[*Then in a triumphant whisper*]
You do, Ned! You do!

DARRELL

[*With dogged stupidity*]
I don't!

[*The front door has been opened.* MARSDEN *appears in
the rear, walks slowly and woodenly like a man in a trance
into the room. He is dressed immaculately in deep
mourning. His face is pale, drawn, haggard with loneliness and grief. His eyes have a dazed look as if he were
still too stunned to comprehend clearly what has happened to him. He does not seem conscious of* DARRELL'S
*presence at first. His shoulders are bowed, his whole
figure droops*]

NINA

[*Thinking—in a strange superstitious panic*]
Black . . . in the midst of happiness . . . black comes
. . . again . . . death . . . my father . . . comes be-
tween me and happiness! . . .
[*Then recovering herself, scornfully*]
You silly coward! . . . it's only Charlie! . . .

[*Then with furious resentment*]

The old fool! . . . what does he mean coming in on us without warning? . . .

MARSDEN

[*Forcing a pitiful smile to his lips*]

Hello, Nina. I know it's an imposition—but—I've been in such a terrible state since Mother—

[*He falters, his face becomes distorted into an ugly mask of grief, his eyes water*]

NINA

[*Immediately sympathetic, gets up and goes to him impulsively*]

There's no question of imposition, Charlie. We were expecting you.

[*She has come to him and put her arms around him. He gives way and sobs, his head against her shoulder*]

MARSDEN

[*Brokenly*]

You don't know, Nina—how terrible—it's terrible!—

NINA

[*Leading him to the chair at center, soothingly*]

I know, Charlie.

[*Thinking with helpless annoyance*]

Oh, dear, what can I say? . . . his mother hated me . . . I'm not glad she's dead . . . but neither am I sorry . . .

[*With a trace of contempt*]

Poor Charlie . . . he was so tied to her apron strings . . .

[*Then kindly but condescendingly, comforting him*]

Poor old Charlie!

MARSDEN

[*The words and the tone shock his pride to life. He raises his head and half-pushes her away—resentfully, thinking*]

Poor old Charlie! . . . damn it, what am I to her? . . . her old dog who's lost his mother? . . . Mother hated her . . . no, poor dear Mother was so sweet, she never hated anyone . . . she simply disapproved . . .

[*Coldly*]

I'm all right, Nina. Quite all right now, thank you. I apologize for making a scene.

DARRELL

[*Has gotten up from his chair—with relief—thinking*]

Thank God for Marsden . . . I feel sane again . . .

[*He comes to* MARSDEN—*cordially*]

How are you, Marsden?

[*Then offering conventional consolation, pats* MARSDEN'S *shoulder*]

I'm sorry, Marsden.

MARSDEN

[*Startled, looks up at him in amazement*]

Darrell!

[*Then with instant hostility*]

There's nothing to be sorry about that I can discover!

[*Then as they both look at him in surprise he realizes what he has said—stammeringly*]

I mean—sorry—is hardly the right word—hardly—is it?

NINA

[*Worriedly*]

Sit down, Charlie. You look so tired.

[*He slumps down in the chair at center mechanically.*
NINA *and* DARRELL *return to their chairs.* NINA *looks
across him at* DARRELL—*triumphantly*—*thinking*]
You do love me, Ned! . . .

DARRELL

[*Thinking—answering her look—defiantly*]
I don't love you! . . .

MARSDEN

[*Stares intensely before him. Thinking suspiciously—
morbidly agitated*]
Darrell! . . . and Nina! . . . there's something in this
room! . . . something disgusting! . . . like a brutal,
hairy hand, raw and red, at my throat! . . . stench of
human life! . . . heavy and rank! . . . outside it's April
. . . green buds on the slim trees . . . the sadness of
spring . . . my loss at peace in Nature . . . her sorrow
of birth consoling my sorrow of death . . . something
human and unnatural in this room! . . . love and hate
and passion and possession! . . . cruelly indifferent to
my loss! . . . mocking my loneliness! . . . no longer any
love for me in any room! . . . lust in this room! . . .
lust with a loathsome jeer taunting my sensitive timidi-
ties! . . . my purity! . . . purity? . . . ha! yes, if you
say prurient purity! . . . lust ogling me for a dollar with
oily shoe button Italian eyes! . . .
[*In terror*]
What thoughts! . . . what a low scoundrel you are! . . .
and your mother dead only two weeks! . . . I hate Nina!
. . . that Darrell in this room! . . . I feel their desires!
. . . where is Sam? . . . I'll tell him! . . . no, he
wouldn't believe . . . he's such a trusting fool . . . I
must punish her some other way . . .
[*Remorsefully*]

What? . . . punish Nina? . . . my little Nina? . . . why, I want her to be happy! . . . even with Darrell? . . . it's all so confused! . . . I must stop thinking! . . . I must talk! . . . forget! . . . say something! . . . forget everything! . . .

[*He suddenly bursts into a flood of garrulity*]

Mother asked for you, Nina—three days before the end. She said, "Where is Nina Leeds now, Charlie? When is she going to marry Gordon Shaw?" Her mind was wandering, poor woman! You remember how fond she always was of Gordon. She used to love to watch the football games when he was playing. He was so handsome and graceful, she always thought. She always loved a strong, healthy body. She took such strict care of her own, she walked miles every day, she loved bathing and boating in the summer even after she was sixty, she was never sick a day in her life until—

[*He turns on* DARRELL—*coldly*]

You were right, Doctor Darrell. It was cancer.

[*Then angrily*]

But the doctor you sent me to, and the others he called in could do nothing for her—absolutely nothing! I might just as well have imported some witch doctors from the Solomon Islands! They at least would have diverted her in her last hours with their singing and dancing, but your specialists were a total loss!

[*Suddenly with an insulting, ugly sneer, raising his voice*]

I think you doctors are a pack of God-damned ignorant liars and hypocrites!

NINA

[*Sharply*]

Charlie!

MARSDEN

[*Coming to himself—with a groan—shamefacedly*]

Don't mind me. I'm not myself, Nina. I've been through hell!

[*He seems about to sob—then abruptly springs to his feet, wildly*]

It's this room! I can't stand this room! There's something repulsive about it!

NINA

[*Soothingly*]

I know it's ugly, Charlie. I haven't had a chance to fix it up yet. We've been too broke.

MARSDEN

[*Confusedly*]

Oh, it's all right. I'm ugly, too! Where's Sam?

NINA

[*Eagerly*]

Right upstairs. Go on up. He'll be delighted to see you.

MARSDEN

[*Vaguely*]

Very well.

[*He goes to the door, then stops mournfully*]

But from what I saw on that visit to his home, he doesn't love his mother much. I don't think he'll understand, Nina. He never writes to her, does he?

NINA

[*Uneasily*]

No—I don't know.

MARSDEN

She seemed lonely. He'll be sorry for it some day after she—

[*He gulps*]

Well—

[*He goes*]

NINA

[*In a sudden panic—thinking*]
Sam's mother! . . . "Make my boy, Sammy, happy!"
. . . I promised . . . oh, why did Charlie have to remember her? . . .
[*Then resolutely*]
I can't remember her now! . . . I won't! . . . I've got to be happy! . . .

DARRELL

[*Uneasily trying to force a casual conversation*]
Poor Marsden is completely knocked off balance, isn't he?
[*A pause*]
My mother died when I was away at school. I hadn't seen her in some time, so her death was never very real to me; but in Marsden's case—

NINA

[*With a possessive smile of tolerance*]
Never mind Charlie, Ned. What do I care about Charlie?
I love you! And you love me!

DARRELL

[*Apprehensively, forcing a tone of annoyed rebuke*]
But I don't! And you don't! You're simply letting your romantic imagination run away with you—

[*Showing his jealous resentment in spite of himself*]
—as you did once before with Gordon Shaw!

NINA

[*Thinking*]
He is jealous of Gordon! . . . how wonderful that
is! . . .
[*With provoking calm*]
I loved Gordon.

DARRELL

[*Irritably ignoring this as if he didn't want to hear it*]
Romantic imagination! It has ruined more lives than all the
diseases! Other diseases, I should say! It's a form of insanity!
[*He gets up forcefully and begins to pace about the
room*]
[*Thinking uneasily*]
Mustn't look at her . . . find an excuse and get
away . . . and this time never come back! . . .
[*Avoiding looking at her, trying to argue reasonably—
coldly*]
You're acting foolishly, Nina—and very unfairly. The
agreement we made has no more to do with love than a con-
tract for building a house. In fact, you know we agreed
it was essential that love mustn't enter into it. And it hasn't
in spite of what you say.
[*A pause. He walks about. She watches him*]
[*Thinking*]
She's got to come back to earth! . . . I've got to break
with her! . . . bad enough now! . . . but to go on with
it! . . . what a mess it'd make of all our lives! . . .

NINA

[*Thinking tenderly*]
Let his pride put all the blame on me! . . . I'll accept
it gladly! . . .

DARRELL

[*Irritably*]
Of course, I realize I've been to blame, too. I haven't been
able to be as impersonal as I thought I could be. The trouble
is there's been a dangerous physical attraction. Since I
first met you, I've always desired you physically. I admit
that now.

NINA

[*Smiling tenderly—thinking*]
Oh, he admits that, does he? . . . poor darling! . . .
[*Enticingly*]
And you still do desire me, don't you, Ned?

DARRELL

[*Keeping his back turned to her—roughly*]
No! That part of it is finished!
[NINA *laughs softly, possessively. He whirls around to
face her—angrily*]
Look here! You're going to have the child you wanted,
aren't you?

NINA

[*Implacably*]
My child wants its father!

DARRELL

[*Coming a little toward her—desperately*]
But you're crazy! You're forgetting Sam! It may be

stupid but I've got a guilty conscience! I'm beginning to
think we've wronged the very one we were trying to help!

NINA

You were trying to help me, too, Ned!

DARRELL

[*Stammering*]
Well—all right—let's say that part of it was all right then.
But it's got to stop! It can't go on!

NINA

[*Implacably*]
Only your love can make me happy now! Sam must give me
a divorce so I can marry you.

DARRELL

[*Thinking suspiciously*]
Look out! . . . there it is! . . . marry! . . . own me!
. . . ruin my career! . . .
[*Scornfully*]
Marry? Do you think I'm a fool? Get that out of your
head quick! I wouldn't marry anyone—no matter what!
[*As she continues to look at him with unmoved determi-
nation—pleadingly*]
Be sensible, for God's sake! We're absolutely unsuited to
each other! I don't admire your character! I don't respect
you! I know too much about your past!
[*Then indignantly*]
And how about Sam? Divorce him? Have you forgotten
all his mother told you? Do you mean to say you'd deliber-

ately——? And you expect me to——? What do you think
I am?

NINA

[*Inflexibly*]

You're my lover! Nothing else matters. Yes, I remember
what Sam's mother said. She said, "being happy is the
nearest we can come to knowing what good is." And I'm
going to be happy! I've lost everything in life so far
because I didn't have the courage to take it—and I've hurt
everyone around me. There's no use trying to think of
others. One human being can't think of another. It's impossible.

[*Gently and caressingly*]

But this time I'm going to think of my own happiness—and
that means you—and our child! That's quite enough for
one human being to think of, dear, isn't it?

[*She reaches out and takes his hand. A pause. With her
other hand she gently pulls him around until he is forced
to look into her eyes*]

DARRELL

[*Thinking fascinatedly*]

I see my happiness in her eyes . . . the touch of her
soft skin! . . . those afternoons! . . . God, I was
happy! . . .

[*In a strange dazed voice—as if it were forced out of
him by an impulse stronger than his will*]

Yes, Nina.

NINA

[*In a determined voice*]

I've given Sam enough of my life! And it hasn't made him

happy, not the least bit! So what's the good? And how
can we really know that his thinking our child was his would
do him any good? We can't! It's all guesswork. The
only thing sure is that we love each other.

DARRELL

[*Dazedly*]

Yes.

[*A noise from the hall and* EVANS *comes in from the rear.
He sees their two hands together but mistakes their
meaning.*]

EVANS

[*Genially—with a forced self-confident air*]
Well, Doc, how's the patient? I think she's much better,
don't you—although she won't admit it.

DARRELL

[*At the first sound of* EVANS' *voice, pulls his hand from*
NINA's *as if it were a hot coal—avoiding* EVANS' *eyes,
moving away from her jerkily and self-consciously*]
Yes. Much better.

EVANS

Good!

[*He pats* NINA *on the back. She shrinks away. His
confidence vanishes in a flash*]
[*Thinking miserably*]
Why does she shrink away . . . if I even touch her? . . .

NINA

[*Matter-of-factly*]
I must see how lunch is coming on. You'll stay, of course,
Ned?

DARRELL

[*Struggling—shakenly*]

No, I think I'd better—

[*Thinking desperately*]

Got to go! . . . can't go! . . . got to go! . . .

EVANS

Oh, come on, old man!

NINA

[*Thinking*]

He must stay . . . and after lunch we'll tell Sam. . . .

[*With certainty*]

He'll stay.

[*Meaningly*]

And we want to have a long talk with you after lunch, Sam
—don't we, Ned?

[DARRELL *does not answer. She goes out, right*]

EVANS

[*Vaguely making talk*]

I got Charlie to lie down. He's all in, poor guy.

[*Then trying to face* DARRELL *who keeps looking away
from him*]

What did Nina mean, you want a long talk with me? Or is
it a secret, Ned?

DARRELL

[*Controlling an impulse toward hysterical laughter*]

A secret? Yes, you bet it's a secret!

[*He flings himself in the chair at left, keeping his face
averted*]

[*His thoughts bitter and desperate like a cornered fugitive's*]

This is horrible! . . . Sam thinks I'm finest fellow in
world . . . and I do this to him! . . . as if he hadn't
enough! . . . born under a curse! . . . I finish him!
. . . a doctor! . . . God damn it! . . . I can see his
end! . . . never forgive myself! . . . never forget! . . .
break me! . . . ruin my career! . . .

[*More desperately*]

Got to stop this! . . . while there's time! . . . she
said . . . after lunch, talk . . . she meant, tell him . . .
that means kill him . . . then she'll marry me! . . .

[*Beginning to be angry*]

By God, I won't! . . . she'll find out! . . . smiling! . . .
got me where she wants me! . . . then be as cruel to me
as she is to him! . . . love me? . . . liar! . . . still loves
Gordon! . . . her body is a trap! . . . I'm caught in it!
. . . she touches my hand, her eyes get in mine, I lose
my will! . . .

[*Furiously*]

By God, she can't make a fool of me that way! . . . I'll
go away some place! . . . go to Europe! . . . study!
. . . forget her in work! . . . keep hidden until boat
sails so she can't reach me! . . .

[*He is in a state of strange elation by this time*]

Go now! . . . no! . . . got to spike her guns with
Sam! . . . by God, I see! . . . tell him about baby! . . .
that'll stop her! . . . when she knows I've told him
that, she'll see it's hopeless! . . . she'll stick to him!
. . . poor Nina! . . . I'm sorry! . . . she does love me!
. . . hell! . . . she'll forget! . . . she'll have her child!
. . . she'll be happy! . . . and Sam'll be happy! . . .

[*He suddenly turns to* EVANS *who has been staring at him,
puzzledly—in a whisper*]

Look here, Sam. I can't stay to lunch. I haven't time, I've
got a million things to do. I'm sailing for Europe in a few
days.

EVANS

[*Surprised*]
You're sailing?

DARRELL

[*Very hurriedly*]
Yes—going to study over there for a year or so. I
haven't told anyone. I came out today to say good-bye.
You won't be able to reach me again. I'll be out of town
visiting.

[*Then elatedly*]
And now for your secret! It ought to make you very
happy, Sam. I know how much you've wished for it, so I'm
going to tell you although Nina'll be furious with me. She
was saving it to surprise you with at her own proper
time—

[*Still more elatedly*]
—but I'm selfish enough to want to see you happy before I
go!

EVANS

[*Not daring to believe what he hopes—stammering*]
What—what is it, Ned?

DARRELL

[*Clapping him on the back—with strange joviality*]
You're going to be a father, old scout, that's the secret!
[*Then as* EVANS *just stares at him dumbly in a blissful
satisfaction, he rattles on*]
And now I've got to run. See you again in a year or so.
I've said good-bye to Nina. Good-bye, Sam.
[*He takes his hand and clasps it*]

Good luck! Buckle down to work now! You've got the stuff
in you! When I get back I'll expect to hear you're on the
highroad to success! And tell Nina I'll expect to find you
both happy in your child—both of you, tell her!—happy in
your child! Tell her that, Sam!

> [*He turns and goes to the door*]
> [*Thinking as he goes*]
> That does it! . . . honorably! . . . I'm free! . . .
> [*He goes out—then out the front door—a moment later
> his motor is heard starting—dies away*]

EVANS

> [*Stares after him dumbly in the same state of happy
> stupefaction—mumbles*]

Thank you—Ned.

> [*Thinking disjointedly*]
> Why did I doubt myself? . . . now she loves me . . .
> she's loved me right along . . . I've been a fool . . .
> [*He suddenly falls on his knees*]
> Oh, God, I thank you!
> [NINA *comes in from the kitchen. She stops in amaze-
> ment when she sees him on his knees. He jumps to his
> feet and takes her in his arms with confident happiness
> and kisses her*]

Oh, Nina, I love you so! And now I know you love me!
I'll never be afraid of anything again!

NINA

> [*Bewildered and terror-stricken, trying feebly to push
> him away—thinking*]
> Has he . . . has he gone crazy? . . .
> [*Weakly*]

Sam! What's come over you, Sam?

EVANS

[*Tenderly*]

Ned told me—the secret—and I'm so happy, dear!

[*He kisses her again*]

NINA

[*Stammering*]

Ned told you—what?

EVANS

[*Tenderly*]

That we're going to have a child, dear. You mustn't be sore at him. Why did you want to keep it a secret from me? Didn't you know how happy it would make me, Nina?

NINA

He told you we—we—you, the father—?

[*Then suddenly breaking from him—wildly*]

Ned! Where is Ned?

EVANS

He left a moment ago.

NINA

[*Stupidly*]

Left? Call him back. Lunch is ready.

EVANS

He's gone. He couldn't stay. He's got so much to do getting ready to sail.

NINA

Sail?

EVANS

Didn't he tell you he was sailing for Europe?   He's going
over for a year or so to study.

NINA

A year or so!
          [*Wildly*]
I've got to call him up!   No, I'll go in and see him right now!
          [*She takes a wavering step toward the door*]
          [*Thinking in anguish*]
          Go! . . . go to him! . . . find him! . . . my lover! . . .

EVANS

He won't be there, I'm afraid.   He said we couldn't reach
him, that he'd be visiting friends out of town until he sailed.
          [*Solicitously*]
Why, do you have to see him about something important,
Nina?   Perhaps I could locate—

NINA

          [*Stammering and swaying*]
No.
          [*She stifles an hysterical laugh*]
No, nothing—nothing important—nothing is important—
ha—!
          [*She stifles another laugh—then on the verge of fainting,
          weakly*]
Sam!   Help me—

EVANS

[*Rushes to her, supports her to sofa at right*]
Poor darling! Lie down and rest.
[*She remains in a sitting position, staring blankly before
her. He chafes her wrists*]
Poor darling!
[*Thinking jubilantly*]
Her condition . . . this weakness comes from her condi-
tion! . . .

NINA

[*Thinking in anguish*]
Ned doesn't love me! . . . he's gone! . . . gone forever! . . . like Gordon! . . . no, not like Gordon! . . .
like a sneak, a coward! . . . a liar! . . . oh, I hate
him! . . . O Mother God, please let me hate him! . . .
he must have been planning this! . . . he must have
known it today when he said he loved me! . . .
[*Thinking frenziedly*]
I won't bear it! . . . he thinks he has palmed me off on
Sam forever! . . . and his child! . . . he can't! . . .
I'll tell Sam he was lying! . . . I'll make Sam hate
him! . . . I'll make Sam kill him! . . . I'll promise to
love Sam if he kills him! . . .
[*Suddenly turns to* EVANS—*savagely*]
He lied to you!

EVANS

[*Letting her wrists drop—appalled—stammers*]
You mean—Ned lied about—?

NINA

[*In same tone*]
Ned lied to you!

EVANS

[*Stammers*]

You're not—going to have a child—

NINA

[*Savagely*]

Oh, yes! Oh, yes, I am! Nothing can keep me from that!
But you're—you're—I mean, you . . .

[*Thinking in anguish*]

I can't say that to him! . . . I can't tell him without
Ned to help me! . . . I can't! . . . look at his face!
. . . oh, poor Sammy! . . . poor little boy! . . . poor
little boy! . . .

[*She takes his head and presses it to her breast and begins to weep*]

[*Weeping*]

I mean, you weren't to know about it, Sammy.

EVANS

[*Immediately on the crest again—tenderly*]

Why? Don't you want me to be happy, Nina?

NINA

Yes—yes, I do, Sammy.

[*Thinking strangely*]

Little boy! . . . little boy! . . . one gives birth to little
boys! . . . one doesn't drive them mad and kill them! . . .

EVANS

[*Thinking*]

She's never called me Sammy before . . . someone used
to . . . oh, yes, Mother. . . .

[*Tenderly and boyishly*]

And I'm going to make you happy from now on, Nina. I

tell you, the moment Ned told me, something happened to me! I can't explain it, but—I'll make good now, Nina! I know I've said that before but I was only boasting. I was only trying to make myself think so. But now I say it knowing I can do it!

[*Softly*]

It's because we're going to have a child, Nina. I knew that you'd never come to really love me without that. That's what I was down on my knees for when you came in. I was thanking God—for our baby!

NINA

[*Tremblingly*]

Sammy! Poor boy!

EVANS

Ned said when he came back he'd expect to find us both happy—in our baby. He said to tell you that. You will be happy now, won't you, Nina?

NINA

[*Brokenly and exhaustedly*]

I'll try to make you happy, Sammy.

[*He kisses her, then hides his head on her breast. She stares out over his head. She seems to grow older*]

[*Thinking as if she were repeating the words of some inner voice of life*]

Not Ned's child! . . . not Sam's child! . . . mine! . . . there! . . . again! . . . I feel my child live . . . moving in my life . . . my life moving in my child . . . breathing in the tide I dream and breathe my dream back into the tide . . . God is a Mother. . . .

[*Then with sudden anguish*]
Oh, afternoons . . . dear wonderful afternoons of love
with you, my lover . . . you are lost . . . gone from me
forever! . . .

CURTAIN

SECOND PART
ACT SIX

ACT SIX

Scene: *The same—an evening a little over a year later.
The room has undergone a significant change. There
is a comfortable, homey atmosphere as though now
it definitely belonged to the type of person it was
built for. It has a proud air of modest prosperity.*

It is soon after dinner—about eight o'clock. Evans
*is sitting by the table at left, glancing through a news-
paper at headlines and reading an article here and
there.* Nina *is in the chair at center, knitting a tiny
sweater.* Marsden *is sitting on the sofa at right, holding a book which he pretends to be looking through, but
glancing wonderingly at* Evans *and* Nina.

There is a startling change in Evans. *He is stouter,
the haggard look of worry and self-conscious inferiority
has gone from his face, it is full and healthy and satisfied. There is also, what is more remarkable, a decided
look of solidity about him, of a determination moving
toward ends it is confident it can achieve. He has ma-
tured, found his place in the world.*

The change in Nina *is also perceptible. She looks
noticeably older, the traces of former suffering are
marked on her face, but there is also an expression of
present contentment and calm.*

Marsden *has aged greatly. His hair is gray, his expression one of a deep grief that is dying out into a*

*resignation resentful of itself. He is dressed immacu-
lately in dark tweed.*

NINA

[*Thinking*]
I wonder if there's a draft in the baby's room? . . .
maybe I'd better close the window? . . . oh, I guess it's
all right . . . he needs lots of fresh air . . . little
Gordon . . . he does remind me of Gordon . . . something in his eyes . . . my romantic imagination? . . .
Ned said that . . . why hasn't Ned ever written? . . .
it's better he hasn't . . . how he made me suffer! . . .
but I forgive him . . . he gave me my baby . . . the
baby certainly doesn't look like him . . . everyone says
he looks like Sam . . . how absurd! . . . but Sam makes
a wonderful father . . . he's become a new man in the
past year . . . and I've helped him . . . he asks me
about everything . . . I have a genuine respect for him
now . . . I can give myself without repulsion . . . I am
making him happy . . . I've written his mother I'm
making him happy . . . I was proud to be able to write
her that . . . how queerly things work out! . . . all for
the best . . . and I don't feel wicked . . . I feel
good . . .
[*She smiles strangely*]

MARSDEN

[*Thinking*]
What a change! . . . the last time I was here the air was
poisoned . . . Darrell . . . I was sure he was her lover
. . . but I was in a morbid state . . . why did Darrell
run away? . . . Nina could have got Sam to divorce her
if she really loved Darrell . . . then it's evident she
couldn't have loved him . . . and she was going to have

Sam's baby . . . Darrell's love must have seemed like
treachery . . . so she sent him away . . . that must be
it . . .
[*With satisfaction*]
Yes, I've got it straight now. . . .
[*With contemptuous pity*]
Poor Darrell . . . I have no use for him but I did pity
him when I ran across him in Munich . . . he was going
the pace . . . looked desperate . . .
[*Then gloomily*]
My running away was about as successful as his . . . as
if one could leave one's memory behind! . . . I couldn't
forget Mother . . . she haunted me through every city of
Europe . . .
[*Then irritatedly*]
I must get back to work! . . . not a line written in over
a year! . . . my public will be forgetting me! . . . a
plot came to me yesterday . . . my mind is coming around
again . . . I am beginning to forget, thank God! . . .
[*Then remorsefully*]
No, I don't want to forget you, Mother! . . . but let me
remember . . . without pain! . . .

EVANS

[*Turning over a page of his paper*]
There's going to be the biggest boom before long this country has ever known, or I miss my guess, Nina.

NINA

[*With great seriousness*]
Do you think so, Sammy?

EVANS

[*Decidedly*]
I'm dead sure of it.

NINA

[*With a maternal pride and amusement*]

Dear Sam . . . I can't quite believe in this self-confident
business man yet . . . but I have to admit he's proved
it . . . he asked for more money and they gave it without question . . . they're anxious to keep him . . . they
ought to be . . . how he's slaved! . . . for me and my
baby! . . .

EVANS

[*Has been looking at* MARSDEN *surreptitiously over his
paper*]

Charlie's mother must have hoarded up a half million . . .
he'll let it rot in government bonds . . . wonder what
he'd say if I proposed that he back me? . . . he's always
taken a friendly interest . . . well, it's worth a bet, anyway . . . he'd be an easy partner to handle . . .

MARSDEN

[*Staring at* EVANS *wonderingly*]

What a changed Sam! . . . I preferred him the old way
. . . futile but he had a sensitive quality . . . now he's
brash . . . a little success . . . oh, he'll succeed all
right . . . his kind are inheriting the earth . . . hogging
it, cramming it down their tasteless gullets! . . . and he's
happy! . . . actually happy! . . . he has Nina . . . a
beautiful baby . . . a comfortable home . . . no sorrow,
no tragic memories . . . and I have nothing! . . . but
utter loneliness! . . .

[*With grieving self-pity*]

If only Mother had lived! . . . how horribly I miss
her! . . . my lonely home . . . who will keep house for
me now? . . . it has got to be done sympathetically or
I won't be able to work . . . I must write to Jane . . .
she'll probably be only too glad . . .

[*Turning to* NINA]

I think I'll write to my sister in California and ask her to come on and live with me. She's alone now that her youngest daughter is married, and she has very little money. And my hands are tied as far as sharing the estate with her is concerned. According to Mother's will, I'm cut off too if I give her a penny. Mother never got over her bitter feeling about Jane's marriage. In a way, she was right. Jane's husband wasn't much—no family or position or ability—and I doubt if she was ever happy with him.

[*Sarcastically*]

It was one of those love matches!

NINA

[*Smiling—teasingly*]

There's no danger of your ever making a love match, is there, Charlie?

MARSDEN

[*Wincing—thinking*]

She can't believe any woman could possibly love me! . . .

[*Caustically*]

I trust I'll never make that kind of a fool of myself, Nina!

NINA

[*Teasingly*]

Pooh! Aren't you the superior bachelor! I don't see anything to be so proud of! You're simply shirking, Charlie!

MARSDEN

[*Wincing but forcing a teasing air*]

You were my only true love, Nina. I made a vow of perpetual bachelorhood when you threw me over in Sam's favor!

EVANS

[*Has listened to this last—jokingly*]

Hello! What's this? I never knew you were my hated rival, Charlie!

MARSDEN

[*Dryly*]

Oh—didn't you really?

[*But* EVANS *has turned back to his paper*]

[*Thinking savagely*]

That fool, too! . . . he jokes about it! . . . as if I were the last one in the world he could imagine . . .

NINA

[*Teasingly*]

Well, if I'm responsible, Charlie, I feel I ought to do something about it. I'll pick out a wife for you—guaranteed to suit! She must be at least ten years older than you, large and matronly and placid, and a wonderful cook and housekeeper—

MARSDEN

[*Sharply*]

Don't be stupid!

[*Thinking angrily*]

She picks someone beyond the age! . . . she never imagines sex could enter into it! . . .

NINA

[*Placatingly—seeing he is really angry*]

Why, I was only picking out a type I thought would be good for you, Charlie—and for your work.

MARSDEN

[*Sneeringly—with a meaning emphasis*]
You didn't mention chaste. I couldn't respect a woman who
hadn't respected herself!

NINA

[*Thinking—stung*]
He's thinking of those men in the hospital . . . what a
fool I was ever to tell him! . . .
[*Cuttingly*]
Oh, so you think you deserve an innocent virgin!

MARSDEN

[*Coldly—controlling his anger*]
Let's drop me, if you please.
[*With a look at her that is challenging and malicious*]
Did I tell you I ran into Doctor Darrell in Munich?

NINA

[*Startled—thinking frightenedly and confusedly*]
Ned! . . . he saw Ned! . . . why hasn't he told me be-
fore? . . . why did he look at me like that? . . . does he
suspect? . . .
[*Trying to be calm but stammering*]
You saw—Ned?

MARSDEN

[*With savage satisfaction*]
That struck home! . . . look at her! . . . guilty! . . .
then I was right that day! . . .
[*Casually*]
Yes, I chanced to run into him.

NINA

[*More calmly now*]
Why on earth didn't you tell us before, Charlie?

MARSDEN

[*Coolly*]
Why? Is it such important news? You knew he was there, didn't you? I supposed he'd written you.

EVANS

[*Looking up from his paper—affectionately*]
How was the old scout?

MARSDEN

[*Maliciously*]
He seemed in fine feather—said he was having a gay time. When I saw him he was with a startling looking female— quite beautiful, if you like that type. I gathered they were living together.

NINA

[*Cannot restrain herself—breaks out*]
I don't believe it!

[*Then immediately controlling herself and forcing a laugh*]
I mean, Ned was always so serious-minded it's hard to imagine him messed up in that sort of thing.

[*Thinking in a queer state of jealous confusion*]
Hard to imagine! . . . my lover! . . . oh, pain again!
. . . why? . . . I don't love him now . . . be careful! . . . Charlie's staring at me. . . .

MARSDEN

[*Thinking—jealously*]
Then she did love him! . . . does she still? . . .

[*Hopefully*]
Or is it only pique? . . . no woman likes to lose a man
even when she no longer loves him. . . .
[*With malicious insistence*]
Why is that hard to imagine, Nina? Darrell never struck
me as a Galahad. After all, why shouldn't he have a mis-
tress?
[*Meaningly*]
He has no tie over here to remain faithful to, has he?

NINA

[*Struggling with herself—thinking pitiably*]
He's right . . . why shouldn't Ned? . . . is that why
he's never written? . . .
[*Airily*]
I don't know what ties he has or hasn't got. It's nothing
to me if he has fifty mistresses. I suppose he's no better than
the rest of you.

EVANS

[*Looking over at her—tenderly reproachful*]
That isn't fair, Nina.
[*Thinking proudly*]
I'm proud of that . . . never anyone before her . . .

NINA

[*Looking at him—with real gratitude*]
I didn't mean you, dear.
[*Thinking—proudly*]
Thank God for Sammy! . . . I know he's mine . . . no
jealousy . . . no fear . . . no pain . . . I've found
peace . . .
[*Then distractedly*]
Oh, Ned, why haven't you written? . . . stop it! . . .

what a fool I am! . . . Ned's dead for me! . . . oh, I
hate Charlie! . . . why did he tell me? . . .

MARSDEN

[*Looking at* EVANS—*contemptuously thinking*]
What a poor simpleton Sam is! . . . boasting of his
virtue! . . . as if women loved you for that! . . . they
despise it! . . . I don't want Nina to think I've had no
experiences with women. . . .
[*Mockingly*]
So then it's Sam who is the Galahad, eh? Really, Nina, you
should have him put in the Museum among the prehistoric
mammals!

EVANS

[*Pleased—comes back kiddingly*]
Well, I never had your chances, Charlie! I couldn't run over
to Europe and get away with murder the way you have!

MARSDEN

[*Foolishly pleased—admitting while denying*]
Oh, I wasn't quite as bad as all that, Sam!
[*Scornfully ashamed of himself—thinking*]
Poor sick ass that I am! . . . I want them to think I've
been a Don Juan! . . . how pitiful and disgusting! . . .
I wouldn't have a mistress if I could! . . . if I could? . . .
of course I could! . . . I've simply never cared to de-
grade myself! . . .

NINA

[*Thinking—tormentedly*]
The thought of that woman! . . . Ned forgetting our
afternoons in nights with her! . . . stop these thoughts!

. . . I won't give in to them! . . . why did Charlie want
to hurt me? . . . is he jealous of Ned? . . . Charlie has
always loved me in some queer way of his own . . . how
ridiculous! . . . look at him! . . . he's so proud of being
thought a Don Juan! . . . I'm sure he never even dared
to kiss a woman except his mother! . . .

[*Mockingly*]

Do tell us about all your various mistresses in foreign parts,
Charlie!

MARSDEN

[*In confusion now*]
I—I really don't remember, Nina!

NINA

Why, you're the most heartless person I've ever heard of,
Charlie! Not remember even one! And I suppose there are
little Marsdens—and you've forgotten all about them too!

[*She laughs maliciously—*EVANS *laughs with her*]

MARSDEN

[*Still more confused—with a silly idiotic smirk*]
I can't say about that, Nina. It's a wise father who knows
his own child, you know!

NINA

[*Frightenedly—thinking*]
What does he mean? . . . does he suspect about the baby
too? . . . I must be terribly careful of Charlie! . . .

EVANS

[*Looking up from his paper again*]
Did Ned say anything about coming back?

NINA

[*Thinking—longingly*]
Come back? . . . oh, Ned, how I wish! . . .

MARSDEN

[*Looking at her—meaningly*]
No, he didn't say. I gathered he was staying over indefi-
nitely.

EVANS

I'd sure like to see him again.

NINA

[*Thinking*]
He has forgotten me . .   if he did come, he'd probably
avoid me. . . .

MARSDEN

He spoke of you. He asked if I'd heard whether Nina had
had her baby yet or not. I told him I hadn't.

EVANS

[*Heartily*]
Too bad you didn't know. You could have told him what
a world-beater we've got! Eh, Nina?

NINA

[*Mechanically*]
Yes.

[*Joyfully—thinking*]
Ned asked about my baby! . . . then he hadn't forgotten! . . . if he came back he'd come to see his baby! . . .

EVANS

[*Solicitously*]
Isn't it time to nurse him again?

NINA

[*Starts to her feet automatically*]
Yes, I'm going now.
[*She glances at Marsden, thinking calculatingly*]
I must win Charlie over again . . . I don't feel safe . . .
[*She stops by his chair and takes his hand and looks into
his eyes gently and reproachfully*]

MARSDEN

[*Thinking shamefacedly*]
Why have I been trying to hurt her? . . . my Nina! . . .
I am nearer to her than anyone! . . . I'd give my life to
make her happy! . . .

NINA

[*Triumphantly*]
How his hand trembles! . . . what a fool to be afraid of
Charlie! . . . I can always twist him round my fin-
ger! . . .
[*She runs her hand through his hair, and speaks as though
she were hiding a hurt reproach beneath a joking tone*]
I shouldn't like you any more, do you know it, after you've
practically admitted you've philandered all over Europe!
And I thought you were absolutely true to me, Charlie!

MARSDEN

[*So pleased he can hardly believe his ears*]
Then she did believe me! . . . she's actually hurt! . . .
but I can't let her think . . .

[*With passionate earnestness, clasping her hand in both
of his, looking into her eyes*]

No, Nina! I swear to you!

NINA

[*Thinking—cruelly*]

Pah! . . . how limp his hands are! . . . his eyes are so
shrinking! . . . is it possible he loves me? . . . like that?
. . . what a sickening idea! . . . it seems incestuous
somehow! . . . no, it's too absurd! . . .

[*Smiling, gently releases her hand*]

All right. I forgive you, Charlie.

[*Then matter-of-factly*]

Excuse me, please, while I go up and feed my infant, or we're
due to hear some lusty howling in a moment.

[*She turns away, then impulsively turns back and kisses*
MARSDEN *with real affection*]

You're an old dear, do you know it, Charlie? I don't know
what I'd do without you!

[*Thinking*]

It's true, too! . . . he's my only dependable friend . . .
I must never lose him . . . never let him suspect about
little Gordon . . .

[*She turns to go*]

EVANS

[*Jumping up, throwing his paper aside*]

Wait a second. I'll come with you. I want to say good
night to him.

[*He comes, puts his arm about her waist, kisses her and
they go out together*]

MARSDEN

[*Thinking excitedly*]

I almost confessed I loved her! . . . a queer expression

came over her face . . . what was it? . . . was it satisfaction? . . . she didn't mind? . . . was it pleasure? . . .
then I can hope? . . .

[*Then miserably*]

Hope for what? . . . what do I want? . . . If Nina
were free, what would I do? . . . would I do anything?
. . . would I wish to? . . . what would I offer her? . . .
money? . . . she could get that from others . . . myself? . . .

[*Bitterly*]

What a prize! . . . my ugly body . . . there's nothing in me to attract her . . . my fame? . . . God, what
a shoddy, pitiful! . . . but I might have done something big . . . I might still . . . if I had the courage
to write the truth . . . but I was born afraid . . .
afraid of myself . . . I've given my talent to making
fools feel pleased with themselves in order that they'd
feel pleased with me . . . and like me . . . I'm neither
hated nor loved . . . I'm liked . . . women like me . . .
Nina likes me! . . .

[*Resentfully*]

She can't help letting the truth escape her! . . . "You're
an old dear, do you know it, Charlie?" Oh, yes, I know
it . . . too damned well! . . . dear old Charlie! . . .

[*In anguish*]

Dear old Rover, nice old doggie, we've had him for years,
he's so affectionate and faithful but he's growing old,
he's getting cross, we'll have to get rid of him soon! . . .

[*In a strange rage, threateningly*]

But you won't get rid of me so easily, Nina! . . .

[*Then confusedly and shamefacedly*]

Good God, what's the matter with me! . . . since
Mother's death I've become a regular idiot! . . .

EVANS

[*Comes back from the right, a beaming look of proud parenthood on his face*]

He was sleeping so soundly an earthquake wouldn't have made him peep!

[*He goes back to his chair—earnestly*]

He sure is healthy and husky, Charlie. That tickles me more than anything else. I'm going to start in training him as soon as he's old enough—so he'll be a crack athlete when he goes to college—what I wanted to be and couldn't. I want him to justify the name of Gordon and be a bigger star than Gordon ever was, if that's possible.

MARSDEN

[*With a sort of pity—thinking*]

His is an adolescent mind . . . he'll never grow up . . . well, in this adolescent country, what greater blessing could he wish for? . . .

[*Forcing a smile*]

How about training his mind?

EVANS

[*Confidently*]

Oh, that'll take care of itself. Gordon was always near the top in his studies, wasn't he? And with Nina for a mother, his namesake ought to inherit a full set of brains.

MARSDEN

[*Amused*]

You're the only genuinely modest person I know, Sam.

EVANS

[*Embarrassed*]

Oh—me—I'm the boob of the family.

[*Then hastily*]

Except when it comes to business.   I'll make the money.

[*Confidently*]

And you can bet your sweet life I will make it!

MARSDEN

I'm quite sure of that.

EVANS

[*Very seriously—in a confidential tone*]

I couldn't have said that two years ago—and believed it.
I've changed a hell of a lot!   Since the baby was born, I've
felt as if I had a shot of dynamite in each arm.   They can't
pile on the work fast enough.

[*He grins—then seriously*]

It was about time I got hold of myself.   I wasn't much for
Nina to feel proud about having around the house in those
days.   Now—well—at least I've improved.   I'm not afraid
of my own shadow any more.

MARSDEN

[*Thinking strangely*]

Not to be afraid of one's shadow! . . . that must be the
highest happiness of heaven! . . .

[*Flatteringly*]

Yes, you've done wonders in the past year.

EVANS

Oh, I haven't even started yet.   Wait till I get my chance!

[*Glances at* MARSDEN *sharply, makes up his mind and
leans forward toward him confidentially*]

And I see my real chance, Charlie—lying right ahead, waiting for me to grab it—an agency that's been allowed to run down and go to seed. Within a year or so they'll be willing to sell out cheap. One of their people who's become a good pal of mine told me that in confidence, put it up to me. He'd take it on himself but he's sick of the game. But I'm not! I love it! It's great sport!

> [*Then putting the brake on this exuberance—matter-of-factly*]

But I'll need a hundred thousand—and where will I get it?

> [*Looking at* MARSDEN *keenly but putting on a joking tone*]

Any suggestion you can make, Charlie, will be gratefully received.

MARSDEN

> [*Thinking suspiciously*]
> Does he actually imagine I . . . ? and a hundred thousand, no less! . . . over one-fifth of my entire . . . by Jove, I'll have to throw cold water on that fancy! . . .
> [*Shortly*]

No, Sam, I can't think of anyone. Sorry.

EVANS

> [*Without losing any confidence—with a grin*]
> Check! . . . That's that! . . . Charlie's out . . . till the next time! . . . but I'll keep after him! . . .
> [*Contemplating himself with pride*]
> Gee, I have changed all right! I can remember when a refusal like that would have ruined my confidence for six months!
> [*Heartily*]

Nothing to be sorry about, old man. I only mentioned it on the off chance you might know of someone.

[*Trying a bold closing stroke—jokingly*]

Why don't you be my partner, Charlie? Never mind the hundred thousand. We'll get that elsewhere. I'll bet you might have darn fine original ideas to contribute.

[*Thinking—satisfied*]

There! . . . That'll keep my proposition pinned up in his mind! . . .

[*Then jumping to his feet—briskly*]

What do you say to a little stroll down to the shore and back? Come on—do you good.

[*Taking his arm and hustling him genially toward the door*]

What you need is exercise. You're soft as putty. Why don't you take up golf?

MARSDEN

[*With sudden resistance pulls away—determinedly*]

No, I won't go, Sam. I want to think out a new plot.

EVANS

Oh, all right! If it's a case of work, go to it! See you later.

[*He goes out. A moment later the front door is heard closing*]

MARSDEN

[*Looks after him with a mixture of annoyance and scornful amusement*]

What a fount of meaningless energy he's tapped! . . . always on the go . . . typical terrible child of the age . . . universal slogan, keep moving . . . moving

where? . . . never mind that . . . don't think of ends . . .
the means are the end . . . keep moving! . . .
[*He laughs scornfully and sits down in* Evans' *chair, picking up the paper and glancing at it sneeringly*]
It's in every headline of this daily newer testament . . .
going . . . going . . . never mind the gone . . . we
won't live to see it . . . and we'll be so rich, we can buy
off the deluge anyway! . . . even our new God has His
price! . . . must have! . . . aren't we made in His
image? . . . or vice-versa? . . .
[*He laughs again, letting the paper drop disdainfully—then bitterly*]
But why am I so superior? . . . where am I going? . . .
to the same nowhere! . . . worse! . . . I'm not even
going! . . . I'm there! . . .
[*He laughs with bitter self-pity—then begins to think with amused curiosity*]
Become Sam's partner? . . . there's a grotesque notion!
. . . it might revive my sense of humor about myself, at
least . . . I'm the logical one to help him . . . I helped
him to Nina . . . logical partner . . . partner in
Nina? . . . what inane thoughts! . . .
[*With a sigh*]
No use trying to think out that plot tonight . . . I'll
try to read. . . .
[*He sees the book he has been reading on the couch and gets up to get it. There is a ring from the front door.* Marsden *turns toward it uncertainly. A pause. Then* Nina's *voice calls down the stairs*]

NINA

The maid's out. Will you go to the door, Charlie?

MARSDEN

Surely.

> [*He goes out and opens the front door.   A pause.   Then he can be heard saying resentfully*]

Hello, Darrell.

> [*And someone answering "Hello,* MARSDEN*" and coming in and the door closing*]

NINA

> [*From upstairs, her voice strange and excited*]

Who is it, Charlie?

DARRELL

> [*Comes into view in the hall, opposite the doorway, at the foot of the stairs—his voice trembling a little with suppressed emotion*]

It's I, Nina—Ned Darrell.

NINA

> [*With a glad cry*]

Ned!

> [*Then in a voice which shows she is trying to control herself, and is frightened now*]

I—make yourself at home.   I'll be down—in a minute or two.

> [DARRELL *remains standing looking up the stairs in a sort of joyous stupor.* MARSDEN *stares at him*]

MARSDEN

> [*Sharply*]

Come on in and sit down.

> [DARRELL *starts, comes into the room, plainly getting a grip on himself.* MARSDEN *follows him, glaring at his back with enmity and suspicion.* DARRELL *moves as far away*

from him as possible, sitting down on the sofa at right.
MARSDEN *takes* EVANS' *chair by the table.* DARRELL *is*
pale, thin, nervous, unhealthy looking. There are lines
of desperation in his face, puffy shadows of dissipation
and sleeplessness under his restless, harried eyes. He is
dressed carelessly, almost shabbily. His eyes wander
about the room, greedily taking it in]

DARRELL

[*Thinking disjointedly*]
Here again! . . . dreamed of this house . . . from here,
ran away . . . I've come back . . . my turn to be
happy! . . .

MARSDEN

[*Watching him—savagely*]
Now I know! . . . absolutely! . . . his face! . . . her
voice! . . . they did love each other! . . . they do
now! . . .
[*Sharply*]
When did you get back from Europe?

DARRELL

[*Curtly*]
This morning on the Olympic.
[*Thinking—cautiously*]
Look out for this fellow . . . always had it in for me
. . . like a woman . . . smells out love . . . he sus-
pected before . . .
[*Then boldly*]
Well, who gives a damn now? . . . all got to come out!
. . . Nina wanted to tell Sam . . . now I'll tell him my-
self! . . .

MARSDEN

[*Righteously indignant*]

What has brought him back? . . . what a devilish, cowardly trick to play on poor unsuspecting Sam! . . .

[*Revengefully*]

But I'm not unsuspecting! . . . I'm not their fool! . . .

[*Coldly*]

What brought you back so soon? When I saw you in Munich you weren't intending—

DARRELL

[*Shortly*]

My father died three weeks ago. I've had to come back about his estate.

[*Thinking*]

Lie . . . Father's death just gave me an excuse to myself . . . wouldn't have come back for that . . . came back because I love her! . . . damn his questions! . . . I want to think . . . before I see her . . . sound of her voice . . . seemed to burn inside my head . . . God, I'm licked! . . . no use fighting it . . . I've done my damnedest . . . work . . . booze . . . other women . . . no use . . . I love her! . . . always! . . . to hell with pride! . . .

MARSDEN

[*Thinking*]

He has two brothers . . . they'll probably all share equally . . . his father noted Philadelphia surgeon . . . rich, I've heard . . .

[*With a bitter grin*]

Wait till Sam hears that! . . . he'll ask Darrell to back him . . . and Darrell will jump at it . . . chance to avert suspicion . . . conscience money, too! . . . it's my duty to protect Sam . . .

[*As he hears* NINA *coming down the stairs*]
I must watch them . . . it's my duty to protect Nina
from herself . . . Sam is a simpleton . . . I'm all she
has . . .

DARRELL

[*Hearing her coming—in a panic—thinking*]
Coming! . . . in a second I'll see her! . . .
[*Terrified*]
Does she still love me? . . . she may have forgotten . . .
no, it's my child . . . she can never forget that! . . .
[NINA *comes in from the rear. She has put on a fresh
dress, her hair is arranged, her face newly rouged and
powdered, she looks extremely pretty and this is height-
ened by the feverish state of mind she is in—a mixture
of love, of triumphant egotism in knowing her lover has
come back to her, and of fear and uncertainty in feeling
her new peace, her certainties, her contented absorption
in her child failing her. She hesitates just inside the door,
staring into* DARRELL'S *eyes, thinking a fierce question*]

NINA

Does he still love me? . . .
[*Then triumphantly as she reads him*]
Yes! . . . he does! . . . he does! . . .

DARRELL

[*Who has jumped to his feet—with a cry of longing*]
Nina!

[*Thinking with alarm now*]
She's changed! . . . changed! . . . can't tell if she
loves! . . .
[*He has started to go to her. Now he hesitates*]
[*His voice taking on a pleading uncertain quality*]
Nina!

NINA

[*Thinking triumphantly—with a certain cruelty*]
He loves me! . . . he's mine . . . now more than ever!
. . . he'll never dare leave me again! . . .
[*Certain of herself now, she comes to him and speaks with confident pleasure*]
Hello, Ned! This is a wonderful surprise! How are you?
[*She takes his hand*]

DARRELL

[*Taken aback—confusedly*]
Oh—all right, Nina.
[*Thinking in a panic*]
That tone! . . . as if she didn't care! . . . can't believe
that! . . . she's playing a game to fool Marsden! . . .

MARSDEN

[*Who is watching them keenly—thinking*]
She loves his love for her . . . she's cruelly confident . . .
much as I hate this man I can't help feeling sorry . . . I
know her cruelty . . . it's time I took a hand in this . . .
what a plot for a novel! . . .
[*Almost mockingly*]
Darrell's father died, Nina. He had to come home to see
about the estate.

DARRELL

[*With a glare at MARSDEN—protestingly*]
I was coming home anyway. I only intended to stay a year,
and it's over that since—
[*Intensely*]
I was coming back anyway, Nina!

NINA

[*Thinking with triumphant happiness*]
You dear, you! . . . as if I didn't know that! . . . oh,
how I'd love to take you in my arms! . . .
[*Happily*]
I'm awfully glad you've come, Ned. We've missed you ter-
ribly.

DARRELL

[*Thinking—more and more at sea*]
She looks glad . . . but she's changed . . . I don't under-
stand her . . . "we've missed" . . . that means Sam . . .
what does that mean? . . .
[*Intensely, pressing her hand*]
And I've missed you—terribly!

MARSDEN

[*Sardonically*]
Yes, indeed, Darrell, I can vouch for their missing you—Sam
in particular. He was asking about you only a short while
ago—how things were going with you when I saw you in
Munich.
[*Maliciously*]
By the way, who was the lady you were with that day? She
was certainly startling looking.

NINA

[*Thinking—triumphantly mocking*]
A miss, Charlie! . . . he loves me! . . . what do I care
about that woman? . . .
[*Gaily*]
Yes, who was the mysterious beauty, Ned? Do tell us!
[*She moves away from him and sits down at center.
DARRELL remains standing*]

DARRELL

[*Glaring at* MARSDEN, *sullenly*]

Oh, I don't remember—

[*Thinking apprehensively with a bitter resentment*]
She doesn't give a damn! . . . if she loved me she'd be
jealous! . . . but she doesn't give a damn! . . .

[*He blurts out resentfully at* NINA]

Well, she was my mistress—for a time—I was lonely.

[*Then with sudden anger turning on* MARSDEN]

But what's all this to you, Marsden?

MARSDEN

[*Coolly*]

Absolutely nothing. Pardon me. It was a tactless question.

[*Then with continued open malice*]

But I was starting to say how Sam had missed you, Darrell.
It's really remarkable. One doesn't encounter such friendship often in these slack days. Why, he'd trust you with
anything!

NINA

[*Wincing—thinking*]

That hurts . . . hurts Ned . . . Charlie is being cruel!
. . .

DARRELL

[*Wincing—in a forced tone*]

And I'd trust Sam with anything.

MARSDEN

Of course. He is a person one can trust. They are rare.
You're going to be amazed at the change in Sam, Darrell.
Isn't he, Nina? He's a new man. I never saw such energy.

If ever a man was bound for success Sam is. In fact, I'm so confident he is that as soon as he thinks the time is ripe to start his own firm I'm going to furnish the capital and become his silent partner.

DARRELL

[*Puzzled and irritated—thinking confusedly*]
What's he driving at? . . . why doesn't he get the hell out and leave us alone? . . . but I'm glad Sam is on his feet . . . makes it easier to tell him the truth. . . .

NINA

[*Thinking—worriedly*]
What's Charlie talking about? . . . it's time I talked to Ned . . . Oh, Ned, I do love you! . . . you can be my lover! . . . we won't hurt Sam! . . . he'll never know! . . .

MARSDEN

Yes, ever since the baby was born Sam's been another man— in fact, ever since he knew there was going to be a baby, isn't it, Nina?

NINA

[*Agreeing as if she had only half-heard him*]
Yes.

[*Thinking*]
Ned's baby! . . . I must talk to him about our baby. . . .

MARSDEN

Sam is the proudest parent I've ever seen!

NINA

[*As before*]

Yes, Sam makes a wonderful father, Ned.

[*Thinking*]

Ned doesn't care for children . . . I know what you're
hoping, Ned . . . but if you think I'm going to take Sam's
baby from him, you're mistaken! . . . or if you think I'll
run away with you and leave my baby . . .

MARSDEN

[*With the same strange driving insistence*]

If anything happened to that child I actually believe Sam
would lose his reason! Don't you think so, Nina?

NINA

[*With emphasis*]

I know I'd lose mine! Little Gordon has become my whole
life.

DARRELL

[*Thinking—with a sad bitter irony*]

Sam . . . wonderful father . . . lose his reason . . . little Gordon! . . . Nina called my son after Gordon! . . .
romantic imagination! . . . Gordon is still her lover! . . .
Gordon, Sam and Nina! . . . and my son! . . . closed
corporation! . . . I'm forced out! . . .

[*Then rebelling furiously*]

No! . . . not yet, by God! . . . I'll smash it up! . . .
I'll tell Sam the truth no matter what! . . .

NINA

[*Thinking with a strange calculation*]

I couldn't find a better husband than Sam . . . and I
couldn't find a better lover than Ned . . . I need them
both to be happy . . .

MARSDEN

[*With sudden despairing suspicion*]

Good God . . . after all, is it Sam's child? . . . mightn't it be Darrell's! . . . why have I never thought of that? . . . No! . . . Nina couldn't be so vile! . . . to go on living with Sam, pretending . . . and, after all, why should she, you fool? . . . there's no sense! . . . she could have gone off with Darrell, couldn't she? . . . Sam would have given her a divorce . . . there was no possible reason for her staying with Sam, when she loved Darrell, unless exactly because this was Sam's baby . . . for its sake . . .

[*Hectically relieved*]

Of course! . . . of course! . . . that's all right! . . . I love that poor baby now! . . . I'll fight for its sake against these two! . . .

[*Smilingly gets to his feet—thinking*]

I can leave them alone now . . . for they won't be alone, thanks to me! . . . I leave Sam and his baby in this room with them . . . and their honor . . .

[*Suddenly raging*]

Their honor! . . . what an obscene joke! . . . the honor of a harlot and a pimp! . . . I hate them! . . . if only God would strike them dead! . . . now! . . . and I could see them die! . . . I would praise His justice! . . . His kindness and mercy to me! . . .

NINA

[*Thinking—with horrified confusion*]

Why doesn't Charlie go? . . . What is he thinking? . . . I suddenly feel afraid of him! . . .

[*She gets to her feet with a confused pleading cry*]

Charlie!

MARSDEN

[*Immediately urbane and smiling*]

It's all right. I'm going out to find Sam. When he knows you're here he'll come on the run, Darrell.

[*He goes to the door. They watch him suspiciously*]
And you two probably have a lot to talk over.

[*He chuckles pleasantly and goes into the hall—mockingly warning*]
We'll be back before long.

[*The front door is heard slamming.* NINA *and* DARRELL *turn and look at each other guiltily and frightenedly. Then he comes to her and takes both of her hands uncertainly*]

DARRELL

[*Stammeringly*]
Nina—I—I've come back to you—do you—do you still care—Nina?

NINA

[*Giving way to his love passionately, as if to drown her fears*]
I love you, Ned!

DARRELL

[*Kisses her awkwardly—stammering*]
I—I didn't know—you seemed so cold—damn Marsden—he suspects, doesn't he?—but it makes no difference now, does it?

[*Then in a flood of words*]
Oh, it's been hell, Nina! I couldn't forget you! Other women—they only made me love you more! I hated them and loved you even at the moment when—that's honest! It was always you in my arms—as you used to be—those afternoons—God, how I've thought of them—lying awake—recalling every word you said, each movement, each ex-

pression on your face, smelling your hair, feeling your soft
body—

[*Suddenly taking her in his arms and kissing her again
and again—passionately*]

Nina! I love you so!

NINA

And I've longed for you so much! Do you think I've forgotten those afternoons?

[*Then in anguish*]

Oh, Ned, why did you run away? I can never forgive that!
I can never trust you again!

DARRELL

[*Violently*]

I was a fool! I thought of Sam! And that wasn't all! Oh,
I wasn't all noble, I'll confess! I thought of myself and my
career! Damn my career! A lot of good that did it! I
didn't study! I didn't live! I longed for you—and suffered!
I paid in full, believe me, Nina! But I know better now!
I've come back. The time for lying is past! You've got to
come away with me!

[*He kisses her*]

NINA

[*Letting herself go, kissing him passionately*]

Yes! My lover!

[*Then suddenly resisting and pushing him away*]

No! You're forgetting Sam—and Sam's baby!

DARRELL

[*Staring at her wildly*]

Sam's baby? Are you joking? Ours, you mean! We'll
take him with us, of course!

NINA

[Sadly]

And Sam?

DARRELL

Damn Sam! He's got to give you a divorce! Let him be generous for a change!

NINA

[Sadly but determinedly]

He would be. You must be just to Sam. He'd give his life for my happiness. And this would mean his life. Could we be happy then? You know we couldn't! And I've changed, Ned. You've got to realize that. I'm not your old mad Nina. I still love you. I will always love you. But now I love my baby too. His happiness comes first with me!

DARRELL

But—he's mine, too!

NINA

No! You gave him to Sam to save Sam!

DARRELL

To hell with Sam! It was to make you happy!

NINA

So I could make Sam happy! That was in it too! I was sincere in that, Ned! If I hadn't been, I could never have gone to you that first day—or if I had, I'd never have forgiven myself. But as it is I don't feel guilty or wicked. I have made Sam happy! And I'm proud! I love Sam's

happiness! I love the devoted husband and father in him!
And I feel it's his baby—that we've made it his baby!

DARRELL

[*Distractedly*]
Nina! For God's sake! You haven't come to love Sam,
have you? Then—I'll go—I'll go away again—I'll never
come back—I tried not to this time—but I had to, Nina!

NINA

[*Taking him in her arms—with sudden alarm*]
No, don't go away, Ned—ever again. I don't love Sam! I
love you!

DARRELL

[*Miserably*]
But I don't understand! Sam gets everything—and I have
nothing!

NINA

You have my love!
[*With a strange, self-assured smile at him*]
It seems to me you're complaining unreasonably!

DARRELL

You mean—I can be—your lover again?

NINA

[*Simply, even matter-of-factly*]
Isn't that the nearest we can come to making everyone
happy? That's all that counts.

DARRELL

[*With a harsh laugh*]
And is that what you call playing fair to Sam?

NINA

[*Simply*]
Sam will never know. The happiness I have given him has
made him too sure of himself ever to suspect me now. And
as long as we can love each other without danger to him, I
feel he owes that to us for all we've done for him.
[*With finality*]
That's the only possible solution, Ned, for all our sakes,
now you've come back to me.

DARRELL

[*Repulsed*]
Nina! How can you be so inhuman and calculating!

NINA

[*Stung—mockingly*]
It was you who taught me the scientific approach, Doctor!

DARRELL

[*Shrinking back from her—threateningly*]
Then I'll leave again! I'll go back to Europe! I won't en-
dure—!
[*Then in a queer, futile rage*]
You think I'll stay—to be your lover—watching Sam with
my wife and my child—you think that's what I came back to
you for? You can go to hell, Nina!

NINA

[*Calmly—sure of him*]
But what else can I do, Ned?
[*Then warningly*]
I hear them coming, dear. It's Sam, you know.

DARRELL

[*In a frenzy*]
What else can you do? Liar! But I can do something else!
I can smash your calculating game for you! I can tell Sam
—and I will—right now—by God, I will!

NINA

[*Quietly*]
No. You won't, Ned. You can't do that to Sam.

DARRELL

[*Savagely*]
Like hell I can't!
[*The front door is opened.* EVANS' *voice is immediately
heard, even before he bounds into the room. He rushes
up to* NED *hilariously, shakes his hand and pounds his
back, oblivious to* DARRELL's *wild expression*]

EVANS

You old son of a gun! Why didn't you let a guy know you
were coming? We'd have met you at the dock, and brought
the baby. Let me have a look at you! You look thinner.
We'll fatten you up, won't we, Nina? Let us do the prescribing this time! Why didn't you let us know where you were,
you old bum? We wanted to write you about the baby. And
I wanted to boast about how I was getting on! You're the

only person in the world—except Nina and Charlie—I would boast about that to.

NINA

[*Affectionately*]
Mercy, Sam, give Ned a chance to get a word in!
[*Looking at* NED *pityingly but challengingly*]
He wants to tell you something, Sam.

DARRELL

[*Crushed—stammers*]
No—I mean, yes—I want to tell you how damn glad I am . . .
[*He turns away, his face is screwed up in his effort to hold back his tears*]
[*Thinking miserably*]
I can't tell him! . . . God damn him, I can't! . . .

NINA

[*With a strange triumphant calm*]
There! . . . that's settled for all time! . . . poor Ned! . . . how crushed he looks! . . . I mustn't let Sam look at him! . . .
[*She steps between them protectingly*]
Where's Charlie, Sam?

MARSDEN

[*Appearing from the hall*]
Here, Nina.   Always here!
[*He comes to her, smiling with assurance*]

NINA

[*Suddenly with a strange unnatural elation—looking from one to the other with triumphant possession*]

Yes, you're here, Charlie—always! And you, Sam—and Ned!

[*With a strange gaiety*]
Sit down, all of you! Make yourselves at home! You are my three men! This is your home with me!

[*Then in a strange half-whisper*]
Ssshh! I thought I heard the baby. You must all sit down and be very quiet. You must not wake our baby.

[*Mechanically the three sit down, careful to make no noise—*Evans *in his old place by the table,* Marsden *at center,* Darrell *on the sofa at right. They sit staring before them in silence.* Nina *remains standing, dominating them, a little behind and to the left of* Marsden]

DARRELL

[*Thinking abjectly*]
I couldn't! . . . there are things one may not do and live with oneself afterwards . . . there are things one may not say . . . memory is too full of echoes! . . . there are secrets one must not reveal . . . memory is lined with mirrors! . . . he was too happy! . . . to kill happiness is a worse murder than taking life! . . . I gave him that happiness! . . . Sam deserves my happiness! . . . God bless you, Sam! . . .

[*Then in a strange objective tone—thinking*]
My experiment with the guinea pigs has been a success . . . the ailing ones, Sam, and the female, Nina, have been restored to health and normal function . . . only the other male, Ned, seems to have suffered deterioration.
. . .

[*Then bitterly humble*]
Nothing left but to accept her terms . . . I love her . . . I can help to make her happy . . . half a loaf is better . . . to a starving man. . . .

[*Glancing over at* EVANS—*bitterly gloating*]
And your child is mine! . . . your wife is mine! . . .
your happiness is mine! . . . may you enjoy my happiness, her husband! . . .

EVANS

[*Looking at* DARRELL *affectionately*]
Sure good to see Ned again . . . a real friend if there
ever was one . . . looks blue about something . . . oh,
that's right, Charlie said his old man had kicked in . . .
his old man was rich . . . that's an idea . . . I'll bet he'd
put up that capital . . .
[*Then ashamed of himself*]
Aw hell, what's the matter with me? . . . he's no sooner
here than I start . . . he's done enough . . . forget
it! . . . now anyway . . . he looks pretty dissipated . . .
too many women . . . ought to get married and settle
down . . . tell him that if I didn't think he'd laugh at
me giving him advice . . . but he'll soon realize I'm not
the old Sam he knew . . . I suppose Nina's been boasting about that already . . . she's proud . . . she's helped
me . . . she's a wonderful wife and mother . . .
[*Looking up at her—solicitously*]
She acted a bit nervous just now . . . queer . . . like
she used to . . . haven't noticed her that way in a long
time . . . suppose it's the excitement of Ned turning up
. . . mustn't let her get over-excited . . . bad for the
baby's milk. . . .

MARSDEN

[*Glancing furtively over his shoulder at* NINA—*brood-
ingly thinking*]
She's the old queer Nina now . . . the Nina I could
never fathom . . . her three men! . . . and we are! . . .
I? . . . yes, more deeply than either of the others since

I serve for nothing . . . a queer kind of love, maybe . . .
I am not ordinary! . . . our child . . . what could she
mean by that? . . . child of us three? . . . on the surface, that's insane . . . but I felt when she said it
there was something in it . . . she has strange devious
intuitions that tap the hidden currents of life . . . dark
intermingling currents that become the one stream of
desire . . . I feel, with regard to Nina, my life queerly
identified with Sam's and Darrell's . . . her child is the
child of our three loves for her . . . I would like to believe that . . . I would like to be her husband in a
sense . . . and the father of a child, after my fashion
. . . I could forgive her everything . . . permit everything . . .

[*Determinedly*]

And I do forgive! . . . and I will not meddle hereafter
more than is necessary to guard her happiness, and Sam's
and our baby's . . . as for Darrell, I am no longer
jealous of him . . . she is only using his love for her
own happiness . . . he can never take her away from
me! . .

NINA

[*More and more strangely triumphant*]

My three men! . . . I feel their desires converge in me!
. . . to form one complete beautiful male desire which
I absorb . . . and am whole . . . they dissolve in me,
their life is my life . . . I am pregnant with the
three! . . . husband! . . . lover! . . . father! . . . and
the fourth man! . . . little man! . . . little Gordon!
. . . he is mine too! . . . that makes it perfect! . . .

[*With an extravagant suppressed exultance*]

Why, I should be the proudest woman on earth! . . . I
should be the happiest woman in the world! . . .

[*Then suppressing an outbreak of hysterical triumphant laughter only by a tremendous effort*]
Ha-ha . . . only I better knock wood . . .
[*She raps with both knuckles in a fierce tattoo on the table*]
before God the Father hears my happiness! . . .

EVANS

[*As the three turn to her—anxiously*]
Nina? What's the matter?

NINA

[*Controlling herself with a great effort comes to him—forcing a smile—puts her arms around him affectionately*]
Nothing, dear. Nerves, that's all. I've gotten over-tired, I guess.

EVANS

[*Bullying her—with loving authority*]
Then you go right to bed, young lady! We'll excuse you.

NINA

[*Quietly and calmly now*]
All right, dear. I guess I do need to rest.
[*She kisses him as she might kiss a big brother she loved —affectionately*]
Good night, you bossy old thing, you!

EVANS

[*With deep tenderness*]
Good night, darling.

NINA

[*She goes and kisses Charlie dutifully on the cheek as she might her father—affectionately*]
Good night, Charlie.

MARSDEN

[*With a touch of her father's manner*]

That's a good girl! Good night, dear.

NINA

[*She goes and kisses* DARRELL *lovingly on the lips as she would kiss her lover*]

Good night, Ned.

DARRELL

[*Looks at her with grateful humility*]

Thank you. Good night.

[*She turns and walks quietly out of the room. The eyes of the three men follow her.*]

CURTAIN

ACT SEVEN

ACT SEVEN

SCENE: *Nearly eleven years later. The sitting room of the* EVANS' *apartment on Park Avenue, New York City —a room that is a tribute to* NINA's *good taste. It is a large, sunny room, the furniture expensive but extremely simple. The arrangement of the furniture shown is as in previous scenes except there are more pieces. Two chairs are by the table at left. There is a smaller table at center, and a chaise longue. A large, magnificently comfortable sofa is at right.*

It is about one in the afternoon of a day in early fall. NINA *and* DARRELL *and their son,* GORDON, *are in the room.* NINA *is reclining on the chaise longue watching* GORDON *who is sitting on the floor near her, turning over the pages of a book.* DARRELL *is sitting by the table at left, watching* NINA.

NINA *is thirty-five, in the full bloom of her womanhood. She is slimmer than in the previous scene. Her skin still retains a trace of summer tan and she appears in the pink of physical condition. But as in the first act of the play, there is beneath this a sense of great mental strain. One notices the many lines in her face at second glance. Her eyes are tragically sad in repose and her expression is set and masklike.*

GORDON *is eleven—a fine boy with, even at this age, the figure of an athlete. He looks older than he is. There*

239

is a grave expression to his face. His eyes are full of a quick-tempered sensitiveness. He does not noticeably resemble his mother. He looks nothing at all like his father. He seems to have sprung from a line distinct from any of the people we have seen.

DARRELL *has aged greatly. His hair is streaked with gray. He has grown stout. His face is a bit jowly and puffy under the eyes. The features have become blurred. He has the look of a man with no definite aim or ambition to which he can relate his living. His eyes are embittered and they hide his inner self-resentment behind a pose of cynical indifference.*

GORDON

[*Thinking as he plays—resentfully*]
I wish Darrell'd get out of here! . . . why couldn't Mother let me run my own birthday? . . . I'd never had him here, you bet! . . . what's he always hanging 'round for? . . . why don't he go off on one of his old trips again . . . last time he was gone more'n a year . . . I was hoping he'd died! . . . what makes Mother like him so much? . . . she makes me sick! . . . I'd think she'd get sick of the old fool and tell him to get out and never come back! . . . I'd kick him out if I was big enough! . . . it's good for him he didn't bring me any birthday present or I'd smash it first chance I got! . . .

NINA

[*Watching him—brooding with loving tenderness—sadly*]
No longer my baby . . . my little man . . . eleven . . . I can't believe it . . . I'm thirty-five . . . five years

more . . . at forty a woman has finished living . . . life
passes by her . . . she rots away in peace! . . .

[*Intensely*]

I want to rot away in peace! . . . I'm sick of the fight
for happiness! . . .

[*Smiling with a wry amusement at herself*]

What ungrateful thoughts on my son's birthday! . . . my
love for him has been happiness . . . how handsome he
is! . . . not at all like Ned . . . when I was carrying
him I was fighting to forget Ned . . . hoping he might
be like Gordon . . . and he is . . . poor Ned, I've made
him suffer a great deal . . . !

[*She looks over at* DARRELL—*self-mockingly*]

My lover! . . . so very rarely now, those interludes
of passion . . . what has bound us together all these
years?. . . love? . . . if he could only have been contented with what I was able to give him! . . . but he
has always wanted more . . . yet never had the courage
to insist on all or nothing . . . proud without being proud
enough! . . . he has shared me for his comfort's sake
with a little gratitude and a big bitterness . . . and sharing me has corrupted him! . . .

[*Then bitterly*]

No, I can't blame myself! . . . no woman can make a
man happy who has no purpose in life! . . . why did he
give up his career? . . . because I had made him
weak? . . .

[*With resentful scorn*]

No, it was I who shamed him into taking up biology and
starting the station at Antigua . . . if I hadn't he'd simply have hung around me year after year, doing nothing . . .

[*Irritatedly*]

Why does he stay so long? . . . over six months . . . I
can't stand having him around me that long any more!

. . . why doesn't he go back to the West Indies? . . . I
always get a terrible feeling after he's been back a while
that he's waiting for Sam to die! . . . or go insane! . . .

DARRELL

[*Thinking—with an apathetic bitterness*]
What is she thinking? . . . we sit together in silence,
thinking . . . thoughts that never know the other's
thoughts . . . our love has become the intimate thinking
together of thoughts that are strangers . . . our love!
. . . well, whatever it is that has bound us together, it's
strong! . . . I've broken with her, run away, tried to
forget her . . . running away to come back each time
more abject! . . . or, if she saw there was some chance
I might break loose, she'd find some way to call me
back . . . and I'd forget my longing for freedom, I'd
come wagging my tail . . . no, guinea pigs have no tails
. . . I hope my experiment has proved something! . . .
Sam . . . happy and wealthy . . . and healthy! . . . I
used to hope he'd break down . . . I'd watch him and
read symptoms of insanity into every move he made . . .
despicable? . . . certainly, but love makes one either
noble or despicable! . . . he only grew healthier . . .
now I've given up watching him . . . almost entirely
. . . now I watch him grow fat and I laugh! . . . the
huge joke has dawned on me! . . . Sam is the only normal one! . . . we lunatics! . . . Nina and I! . . . have
made a sane life for him out of our madness! . . .
[*Watching* NINA—*sadly*]
Always thinking of her son . . . well, I gave him to
her . . . Gordon . . . I hate that name . . . why do I
continue hanging around here? . . . each time after a
few months my love changes to bitterness . . . I blame
Nina for the mess I've made of life . . .

NINA

[*Suddenly turning on him*]

When are you going back to the West Indies, Ned?

DARRELL

[*Determinedly*]

Soon!

GORDON

[*Stops playing to listen—thinking*]

Gosh, I'm glad! . . . How soon, I wonder? . . .

NINA

[*With a trace of a sneer*]

I don't see how you can afford to leave your work for such long periods. Don't you grow rusty?

DARRELL

[*Looking at her meaningly*]

My life work is to rust—nicely and unobtrusively!

[*He smiles mockingly*]

NINA

[*Sadly—thinking*]

To rot away in peace . . . that's all he wants now, too! . . . and this is what love has done to us! . . .

DARRELL

[*Bitterly*]

My work was finished twelve years ago. As I believe you know, I ended it with an experiment which resulted so successfully that any further meddling with human lives would have been superfluous!

NINA

[*Pityingly*]

Ned!

DARRELL

[*Indifferent and cynical*]

But you meant my present dabbling about. You know
better than to call that work. It's merely my hobby. Our
backing Sam has made Marsden and me so wealthy that
we're forced to take up hobbies. Marsden goes in for his
old one of dashing off genteel novels, while I play at biology.
Sam argued that golf would be healthier and less nonsensical
for me, but you insisted on biology. And give it its due, it
has kept me out in the open air and been conducive to travel-
ling and broadening my mind!

[*Then forcing a smile*]

But I'm exaggerating. I really am interested, or I'd never
keep financing the Station. And when I'm down there I do
work hard, helping Preston. He's doing remarkable work
already, and he's still in his twenties. He'll be a big man—

[*His bitterness cropping up again*]

at least if he takes my advice and never carries his experi-
ments as far as human lives!

NINA

[*In a low voice*]

How can you be so bitter, Ned—on Gordon's birthday?

DARRELL

[*Thinking cynically*]

She expects me to love the child she deliberately took
from me and gave to another man! . . . no, thank you,

Nina! . . . I've been hurt enough! . . . I'll not leave
myself open there! . . .
[*Regarding his son bitterly*]
Every day he gets more like Sam, doesn't he?

GORDON

[*Thinking*]
He's talking about me . . . he better look out! . . .

NINA

[*Resentfully*]
I don't think Gordon resembles Sam at all. He reminds me
a great deal of his namesake.

DARRELL

[*Touched on a sore spot—with a nasty laugh—cuttingly*]
Gordon Shaw? Not the slightest bit in the world! And you
ought to thank God he doesn't! It's the last thing I'd want
wished on a boy of mine—to be like that rah-rah hero!

GORDON

[*Thinking contemptuously*]
Boy of his! . . . He hasn't got a boy! . . .

NINA

[*Amused and pleased by his jealousy*]
Poor Ned! . . . isn't he silly? . . . at his age, after all
we've been through, to still feel jealous . . .

DARRELL

I'd much rather have him
[*Pointing to* GORDON]
grow up to be an exact duplicate of the esteemed Samuel!

GORDON

[*Thinking resentfully*]
He's always making fun of my father! . . . he better
look out! . . .

DARRELL

[*More and more mockingly*]
And what could be fairer? The good Samuel is an A one
success. He has a charming wife and a darling boy, and a
Park Avenue apartment and a membership in an expensive
golf club. And, above all, he rests so complacently on the
proud assurance that he is self-made!

NINA

[*Sharply*]
Ned! You ought to be ashamed! You know how grateful
Sam has always been to you!

DARRELL

[*Bitingly*]
Would he be grateful if he knew how much I'd really done for
him?

NINA

[*Sternly*]
Ned!

GORDON

[*Suddenly jumps up and confronts DARRELL, his fists
clenched, trembling with rage, stammers*]
You—shut up—making fun of my father!

NINA

[*In dismay*]
Gordon!

DARRELL

[*Mockingly*]

My dear boy, I wouldn't make fun of your father for the world!

GORDON

[*Baffledly—his lips trembling*]

You—you did, too!

[*Then intensely*]

I hate you!

NINA

[*Shocked and indignant*]

Gordon! How dare you talk like that to your Uncle Ned!

GORDON

[*Rebelliously*]

He's not my uncle! He's not my anything!

NINA

Not another word or you'll be punished, whether it's your birthday or not! If you can't behave better than that, I'll have to phone to all your friends they mustn't come here this afternoon, that you've been so bad you can't have a party!

[*Thinking remorsefully*]

Is this my fault? . . . I've done my best to get him to love Ned! . . . but it only makes him worse! . . . it makes him turn against me! . . . turn from me to Sam! . . .

GORDON

[*Sullenly*]

I don't care! I'll tell Dad!

NINA

[*Peremptorily*]

Leave the room! And don't come near me again, do you
hear, until you've apologized to Uncle Ned!

[*Thinking angrily*]

Dad! . . . It's always Dad with him now! . . .

DARRELL

[*Boredly*]

Oh, never mind, Nina!

GORDON

[*Going out—mutters*]

I won't 'pologize—never!

[*Thinking vindictively*]

I hate her too when she sides with him! . . . I don't care
if she is my mother! . . . she has no right! . . .

[*He goes out, rear*]

DARRELL

[*Irritably*]

What if he does hate me? I don't blame him! He suspects
what I know—that I've acted like a coward and a weakling
toward him! I should have claimed him no matter what
happened to other people! Whose fault is it if he hates
me, and I dislike him because he loves another father? Ours!
You gave him to Sam and I consented! All right! Then
don't blame him for acting like Sam's son!

NINA

But he shouldn't say he hates you.

[*Thinking bitterly*]

Sam's! . . . he's becoming all Sam's! . . . I'm getting to
mean nothing! . . .

DARRELL

[*Sardonically*]
Perhaps he realizes subconsciously that I am his father, his
rival in your love; but I'm not his father ostensibly, there are
no taboos, so he can come right out and hate me to his
heart's content!
[*Bitterly*]
If he realized how little you love me any more, he wouldn't
bother!

NINA

[*Exasperatedly*]
Oh, Ned, do shut up! I can't stand hearing those same old
reproaches I've heard a thousand times before! I can't bear
to hear myself making the same old bitter counter-accusa-
tions. And then there'll be the same old terrible scene of hate
and you'll run away—it used to be to drink and women,
now it's to the Station. Or I'll send you away, and then
after a time I'll call you back, because I'll have gotten so
lonely again living this lonely lie of my life, with no one to
speak to except Sam's business friends and their deadly
wives.
[*She laughs helplessly*]
Or else you'll get lonely in your lie a little before I do and
come back again of your own desire! And then we'll kiss
and cry and love each other again!

DARRELL

[*With an ironical grimace*]
Or I might cheat myself into believing I'd fallen in love with

some nice girl and get myself engaged to be married again
as I did once before! And then you'd be jealous again and
have to find some way of getting me to break it off!

NINA

[*Forlornly amused*]
Yes—I suppose the thought of a wife taking you away from
me would be too much—again!
[*Then helplessly*]
Oh, Ned, when are we ever going to learn something about
each other? We act like such brainless fools—with our
love. It's always so wonderful when you first come back,
but you always stay too long—or I always keep you too
long! You never leave before we've come to the ugly bitter
stage when we blame each other!
[*Then suddenly forlornly tender*]
Is it possible you can still love me, Ned?

DARRELL

[*Mournfully smiling*]
I must, or I'd never act this fool way, would I?

NINA

[*Smiling back*]
And I must love you.
[*Then seriously*]
After all, I can never forget that Gordon is the child of
your love, Ned.

DARRELL

[*Sadly*]
You'd better forget that, for his sake and your own. Chil-

dren have sure intuitions. He feels cheated of your love—
by me. So he's concentrating his affections on Sam whose
love he knows is secure, and withdrawing from you.

NINA

[*Frightened—angrily*]
Don't be stupid, Ned! That isn't so at all! I hate you
when you talk that way!

DARRELL

[*Cynically*]
Hate me, exactly. As he does! That's what I'm advising
you to do if you want to keep his love!
[*He smiles grimly*]

NINA

[*Sharply*]
If Gordon doesn't love you it's because you've never made
the slightest attempt to be lovable to him! There's no
earthly reason why he should like you, when you come right
down to it, Ned! Take today, for instance. It's his birthday but you'd forgotten, or didn't care! You never even
brought him a present.

DARRELL

[*With bitter sadness*]
I did bring him a present. It's out in the hall. I bought
him a costly delicate one so he could get full satisfaction and
yet not strain himself when he smashed it, as he's smashed
every present of mine in the past! And I left it out in the
hall, to be given to him after I've gone because, after all, he
is my son and I'd prefer he didn't smash it before my eyes!

[Trying to mock his own emotion back—with savage bitterness]

I'm selfish, you see! I don't want my son to be too happy at my expense, even on his birthday!

NINA

[Tormented by love and pity and remorse]

Ned! For God's sake! How can you torture us like that! Oh, it's too dreadful—what I have done to you! Forgive me, Ned!

DARRELL

[His expression changing to one of pity for her—goes to her and puts his hand on her head—tenderly]

I'm sorry.

[With remorseful tenderness]

Dreadful, what you've done, Nina? Why, you've given me the only happiness I've ever known! And no matter what I may say or do in bitterness, I'm proud—and grateful, Nina!

NINA

[Looks up at him with deep tenderness and admiration]

Dearest, it's wonderful of you to say that!

[She gets up and puts her hands on his shoulders and looks into his eyes—tenderly in a sort of pleading]

Can't we be brave enough—for you to go away—now, on this note—sure of our love—with no ugly bitterness for once?

DARRELL

[Joyfully]

Yes! I'll go—this minute if you wish!

NINA

[*Playfully*]

Oh, you needn't go this minute! Wait and say good-bye to
Sam. He'd be terribly hurt if you didn't.

[*Then seriously*]

And will you promise to stay away two years—even if I
call you back before then—and work this time, really work?

DARRELL

I'll try, Nina!

NINA

And then—surely come back to me!

DARRELL

[*Smiling*]

Surely—again!

NINA

Then good-bye, dear!

[*She kisses him*]

DARRELL

Again!

[*He smiles and she smiles and they kiss again.* GORDON
*appears in the doorway at rear and stands for a moment
in a passion of jealousy and rage and grief, watching
them*]

GORDON

[*Thinking with a strange tortured shame*]

I mustn't see her! . . . pretend I didn't see her! . . .
mustn't never let her know I saw her! . . .

[*He vanishes as silently as he had come*]

NINA

[*Suddenly moving away from* DARRELL, *looking around her uneasily*]

Ned, did you see——? I had the queerest feeling just then that someone——

GORDON

[*His voice sounds from the hall with a strained casualness*]

Mother! Uncle Charlie's downstairs. Shall he come right up?

NINA

[*Startled, her own voice straining to be casual*]

Yes, dear——of course!

[*Then worriedly*]

His voice sounded funny. Did it to you? Do you suppose he——?

DARRELL

[*With a wry smile*]

It's possible. To be on the safe side, you'd better tell him you kissed me good-bye to get rid of me!

[*Then angrily*]

So Marsden's here again! The damned old woman! I simply can't go him any more, Nina! Why Gordon should take such a fancy to that old sissy is beyond me!

NINA

[*Suddenly struck—thinking*]

Why, he's jealous of Gordon liking Charlie! . . .

[*Immediately all affectionate pity*]

Then he must love Gordon a little! . . .

[*Letting her pity escape her*]

Poor Ned!

[*She makes a movement toward him*]

DARRELL

[*Startled and afraid she may have guessed something he doesn't acknowledge to himself*]

What? Why do you say that?

[*Then rudely defensive*]

Don't be silly!

[*Resentfully*]

You know well enough what I've always held against him! I wanted to put up all the money to back Sam when he started. I wanted to do it for Sam's sake—but especially for my child's sake. Why did Marsden absolutely insist on Sam letting him in equally? It isn't that I begrudge him the money he's made, but I know there was something queer in his mind and that he did it intentionally to spite me!

[*From the hallway comes the sound of* MARSDEN'*s voice and* GORDON'*s greeting him vociferously as he lets him into the apartment. As* DARRELL *listens his expression becomes furious again. He bursts out angrily*]

You're letting that old ass spoil Gordon, you fool, you!

[MARSDEN *comes in from the rear, smiling, immaculately dressed as usual. He looks hardly any older except that his hair is grayer and his tall figure more stooped. His expression and the general atmosphere he gives out are more nearly like those of Act One. If not happy, he is at least living in comparative peace with himself and his environment*]

MARSDEN

[*Comes straight to* NINA]

Hello, Nina Cara Nina! Congratulations on your son's birthday!

[*He kisses her*]

He's grown so much bigger and stronger in the two months since I've seen him.

> [*He turns and shakes hands with* DARRELL *coldly—with a trace of a patronizing air*]

Hello, Darrell. Last time I was here you were leaving for the West Indies in a week but I see you're still around.

DARRELL

> [*Furious—with a mocking air*]

And here you are around again yourself! You're looking comfortable these days, Marsden. I hope your sister is well. It must be a great comfort, having her to take your mother's place!

> [*Then with a harsh laugh*]

Yes, we're two bad pennies, eh, Marsden?—counterfeits— fakes—Sam's silent partners!

NINA

> [*Thinking irritably*]

Ned's getting hateful again! . . . Poor Charlie! . . . I won't have him insulted! . . . he's become such a comfort . . . he understands so much . . . without my having to tell him . . .

> [*Looking rebukingly at* DARRELL]

Ned is sailing this week, Charlie.

MARSDEN

> [*Thinking triumphantly*]

He's trying to insult me . . . I know all he means . . . but what do I care what he says . . . she's sending him away! . . . intentionally before me! . . . it means he's finished! . . .

DARRELL

[*Thinking resentfully*]
Is she trying to humiliate me before him? . . . I'll teach her! . . .
[*Then struggling with himself—remorsefully*]
No . . . not this time . . . I promised . . . no quarrel . . . remember . . .
[*Acquiescing—with a pleasant nod to* MARSDEN]
Yes, I'm going this week and I expect to be gone at least two years this time—two years of hard work.

MARSDEN

[*Thinking with scornful pity*]
His work! . . . what a pretense! . . . a scientific dilettante! . . . could anything be more pitiable? . . . poor chap! . . .
[*Perfunctorily*]
Biology must be an interesting study. I wish I knew more about it.

DARRELL

[*Stung yet amused by the other's tone—ironically*]
Yes, so do I wish you did, Marsden! Then you might write more about life and less about dear old ladies and devilish bachelors! Why don't you write a novel about life sometime, Marsden?
[*He turns his back on* MARSDEN *with a glance of repulsion and walks to the window and stares out*]

MARSDEN

[*Confusedly*]
Yes—decidedly—but hardly in my line—
[*Thinking in anguish—picking up a magazine and turning over the pages aimlessly*]

That . . . is . . . true! . . . he's full of poison! . . .
I've never married the word to life! . . . I've been a
timid bachelor of Arts, not an artist! . . . my poor
pleasant books! . . . all is well! . . . is this well, the
three of us? . . . Darrell has become less and less her
lover . . . Nina has turned more and more to me . . .
we have built up a secret life of subtle sympathies and
confidences . . . she has known I have understood about
her mere physical passion for Darrell . . . what woman
could be expected to love Sam passionately? . . . some
day she'll confide all about Darrell to me . . . now that
he's finished . . . she knows that I love her without my
telling . . . she even knows the sort of love it is. . . .
[*Passionately—thinking*]
My love is finer than any she has known! . . . I do not
lust for her! . . . I would be content if our marriage
should be purely the placing of our ashes in the same
tomb . . . our urns side by side and touching one another
. . . could the others say as much, could they love so
deeply? . . .
[*Then suddenly miserably self-contemptuous*]
What! . . . platonic heroics at my age! . . . do I believe a word of that? . . . look at her beautiful eyes!
. . . wouldn't I give anything in life to see them desire
me? . . . and the intimacy I'm boasting about, what
more does it mean than that I've been playing the dear
old Charlie of her girlhood again? . . .
[*Thinking in anguish*]
Damned coward and weakling! . . .

NINA

[*Looking at him—pityingly—thinking*]
What does he always want of me? . . . me? . . . I am
the only one who senses his deep hurt . . . I feel how
life has wounded him . . . is that partly my fault, too?

. . . I have wounded everyone . . . poor Charlie, what
can I do for you? . . . if giving myself to you would
bring you a moment's happiness, could I? . . . the idea
used to be revolting . . . now, nothing about love seems
important enough to be revolting . . . poor Charlie, he
only thinks he ought to desire me! . . . dear Charlie,
what a perfect lover he would make for one's old age!
. . . what a perfect lover when one was past passion!
. . .
[*Then with sudden scornful revulsion*]
These men make me sick! . . . I hate all three of
them! . . . they disgust me! . . . the wife and mistress
in me has been killed by them! . . . thank God, I am
only a mother now! . . . Gordon is my little man, my
only man! . . .
[*Suddenly*]
I've got a job for you, Charlie—make the salad dressing for
lunch. You know, the one I'm so crazy about.

MARSDEN

[*Springs to his feet*]
Righto!
[*He puts his arm about her waist and they go out to-
gether laughingly, without a glance at* DARRELL]

DARRELL

[*Thinking dully*]
I mustn't stay to lunch . . . ghost at my son's feast! . . .
I better go now . . . why wait for Sam? . . . what is
there to say to him I can say? . . . and there's nothing
about him I want to see . . . he's as healthy as a pig
. . . and as sane . . . I was afraid once his mother had
lied to Nina . . . I went upstate and investigated . . .
true, every word of it . . . his great-grandfather, his

grandmother, his father, were all insane . . .
[*Moving uneasily*]
Stop it! . . . time to go when those thoughts come . . .
sail on Saturday . . . not come here again . . . Nina will
soon be fighting Sam for my son's love! . . . I'm better
out of that! . . . O Christ, what a mess it all is! . . .

GORDON

[*Appears in the doorway in rear. He carries a small,
expensive yacht's model of a sloop with the sails set. He
is in a terrific state of conflicting emotions, on the verge
of tears yet stubbornly determined*]
I got to do it! . . . Gosh, it's awful . . . this boat is so
pretty . . . why did it have to come from him? . . . I
can get Dad to buy me another boat . . . but now I
love this one . . . but he kissed Mother . . . she kissed
him . . .
[*He walks up defiantly and confronts* DARRELL *who turns
to him in surprise*]
Hey—Darrell—did you—?
[*He stops chokingly*]

DARRELL

[*Immediately realizing what is coming—thinking with
somber anguish*]
So this has to happen! . . . what I dreaded! . . . my
fate is merciless, it seems! . . .
[*With strained kindliness*]
Did what?

GORDON

[*Growing hard—stammers angrily*]
I found this—out in the hall. It can't be from anybody else.
Is this—your present?

DARRELL

[*Hard and defiant himself*]

Yes.

GORDON

[*In a rage—tremblingly*]

Then—here's what—I think of you!

[*Beginning to cry, he breaks off the mast, bowsprit, breaks the mast in two, tears the rigging off and throws the dismantled hull at DARRELL's feet*]

There! You can keep it!

DARRELL

[*His anger overcoming him for an instant*]

You—you mean little devil, you! You don't get that from me—

[*He has taken a threatening step forward. GORDON stands white-faced, defying him. DARRELL pulls himself up short—then in a trembling voice of deeply wounded affection*]

You shouldn't have done that, son. What difference do I make? It was never my boat. But it was your boat. You should consider the boat, not me. Don't you like boats for themselves? It was a beautiful little boat, I thought. That's why I—

GORDON

[*Sobbing miserably*]

It was awful pretty! I didn't want to do it!

[*He kneels down and gathers up the boat into his arms again*]

Honest I didn't. I love boats! But I hate you!

[*This last with passionate intensity*]

DARRELL

[*Dryly*]
So I've observed.

[*Thinking with angry anguish*]
He hurts, damn him! . . .

GORDON

No, you don't know! More'n ever now! More'n ever!
[*The secret escaping him*]
I saw you kissing Mother! I saw Mother, too!

DARRELL

[*Startled, but immediately forcing a smile*]
But I was saying good-bye. We're old friends. You know
that.

GORDON

You can't fool me! This was different!
[*Explosively*]
It would serve you good and right—and Mother, too—if I
was to tell Dad on you!

DARRELL

Why, I'm Sam's oldest friend. Don't make a little fool
of yourself!

GORDON

You are not his friend. You've always been hanging around
cheating him—hanging around Mother!

DARRELL

Keep still! What do you mean cheating him?

GORDON

I don't know. But I know you aren't his friend. And sometime I'm going to tell him I saw you—

DARRELL

[*With great seriousness now—deeply moved*]
Listen! There are things a man of honor doesn't tell any-
one—not even his mother or father. You want to be a man
of honor, don't you?
[*Intensely*]
There are things we don't tell, you and I!
[*He has put his hand around* GORDON's *shoulder im-
pulsively*]
This is my son! . . . I love him! . . .

GORDON

[*Thinking—terribly torn*]
Why do I like him now? . . . I like him awful! . . .
[*Crying*]
We?—who d'you mean?—I've got honor!—more'n you!—
you don't have to tell me!—I wasn't going to tell Dad anyway, honest I wasn't! We?—what d'you mean, we?—I'm
not like you! I don't want to be ever like you!
[*There is the sound of a door being flung open and shut
and* EVANS' *hearty voice*]

EVANS

[*From the entrance hall*]
Hello, everybody!

DARRELL

[*Slapping* GORDON *on the back*]
Buck up, son! Here he is! Hide that boat or he'll ask questions.

[GORDON *runs and hides the boat under the sofa. When* EVANS *enters,* GORDON *is entirely composed and runs to him joyfully.* EVANS *has grown stouter, his face is heavy now, he has grown executive and used to command, he automatically takes charge wherever he is. He does not look his age except that his hair has grown scanty and there is a perceptible bald spot on top. He is expensively tailored*]

EVANS

[*Hugging* GORDON *to him—lovingly*]

How's the old son? How's the birthday coming along?

GORDON

Fine, Dad!

EVANS

Hello, Ned! Isn't this kid of mine a whopper for his age, though!

DARRELL

[*Smiling strainedly*]

Yes.

[*Writhing—thinking*]

It hurts now! . . . to see my son his son! . . . I've had enough! . . . get out! . . . any excuse! . . . I can phone afterwards! . . . I'll yell out the whole business if I stay! . . .

I was just going, Sam. I've got to step around and see a fellow who lives near—biologist.

[*He has gone to the door*]

EVANS

[*Disappointedly*]

Then you won't be here for lunch?

DARRELL

[*Thinking*]

I'll yell the truth into your ears if I stay a second
longer . . . you damned lunatic! . . .

Can't stay. Sorry. This is important. I'm sailing in a
few days—lots to do—see you later, Sam. So long—
Gordon.

GORDON

[*As he goes out with awkward haste*]

Good-bye—Uncle Ned.

[*Thinking confusedly*]

Why did I call him that when I said I never would? . . .
I know . . . must be because he said he's sailing and
I'm, glad . . .

EVANS

So long, Ned.

[*Thinking—good-naturedly superior*]

Ned and his biology! . . . He takes his hobby pretty
seriously! . . .

[*With satisfaction*]

Well, he can afford to have hobbies now! . . . his in-
vestment with me has made him a pile. . . .

Where's Mother, son?

GORDON

Out in the kitchen with Uncle Charlie.

[*Thinking*]

I hope he never comes back! . . . why did I like him
then? . . . it was only for a second . . . I didn't really
. . . I never could! . . . why does he always call me
Gordon as if he hated to? . . .

EVANS

[*Sitting down at left*]

I hope lunch is ready soon. I'm hungry as the devil, aren't you?

GORDON

[*Absent-mindedly*]

Yes, Dad.

EVANS

Come over here and tell me about your birthday.

[GORDON *comes over.* EVANS *pulls him up on his lap*]

How'd you like your presents? What'd you get from Uncle Ned?

GORDON

[*Evasively*]

They were all dandy.

[*Suddenly*]

Why was I named Gordon?

EVANS

Oh, you know all about that—all about Gordon Shaw. I've told you time and again.

GORDON

You told me once he was Mother's beau—when she was a girl.

EVANS

[*Teasingly*]

What do you know about beaus? You're growing up!

GORDON

Did Mother love him a lot?

EVANS

[*Embarrassedly*]

I guess so.

GORDON

[*Thinking keenly*]

That's why Darrell hates me being called Gordon . . .
he knows Mother loved Gordon better'n she does him . . .
now I know how to get back at him . . . I'll be just like
Gordon was and Mother'll love me better'n him! . . .
And then that Gordon was killed, wasn't he? Am I anything
like him?

EVANS

I hope you are. If when you go to college you can play
football or row like Gordon did, I'll—I'll give you anything
you ask for! I mean that!

GORDON

[*Dreamily*]

Tell me about him again, will you, Dad—about the time
he was stroking the crew and the fellow who was Number
Seven began to crack, and he couldn't see him but he felt him
cracking somehow, and he began talking back to him all the
time and sort of gave him his strength so that when the race
was over and they'd won Gordon fainted and the other
fellow didn't.

EVANS

[*With a fond laugh*]

Why, you know it all by heart! What's the use of my telling
you?

NINA

[*Comes in from the rear while they are talking. She
comes forward slowly*]

[*Thinking resentfully*]

Does he love Sam more than he does me? . . . oh, no, he can't! . . . but he trusts him more! . . . he confides in him more! . . .

GORDON

Did you ever used to fight fellows, Dad?

EVANS

[*Embarrassedly*]

Oh, a little—when I had to.

GORDON

Could you lick Darrell?

NINA

[*Thinking frightenedly*]

Why does he ask that? . . .

EVANS

[*Surprised*]

Your Uncle Ned? What for? We've always been friends.

GORDON

I mean, if you weren't friends, could you?

EVANS

[*Boastfully*]

Oh, yes, I guess so. Ned was never as strong as I was.

NINA

[*Thinking contemptuously*]
Ned is weak. . . .
[*Then apprehensively*]
But you're getting too strong, Sam. . . .

GORDON

But Gordon could have licked you, couldn't he?

EVANS

You bet he could!

GORDON

[*Thinking*]
She must have loved Gordon better'n Dad even! . . .

NINA

[*She comes forward to the chair at center, forcing a
smile*]
What's all this talk about fighting? That's not nice. For
heaven's sake, Sam, don't encourage him—

EVANS

[*Grinning*]
Never mind the women, Gordon. You've got to know how to
fight to get on in this world.

NINA

[*Thinking pityingly*]
You poor booby! . . . how brave you are now! . . .
[*Softly*]
Perhaps you're right, dear.
[*Looking around*]
Has Ned gone?

GORDON

[*Defiantly*]
Yes—and he's not coming back—and he's sailing soon!

NINA

[*With a shudder*]
Why does he challenge me that way? . . . and cling to
Sam? . . . he must have seen Ned and me . . . he
doesn't offer to come to my lap . . . he used to . . . Ned
was right . . . I've got to lie to him . . . get him back
. . . here . . . on my lap! . . .
[*With a sneer—to* EVANS]
I'm glad Ned's gone. I was afraid he was going to be on our
hands all day.

GORDON

[*Eagerly, half-getting down from his father's lap*]
You're glad—?
[*Then cautiously thinking*]
She's cheating . . . I saw her kiss him. . . .

NINA

Ned's getting to be an awful bore. He's so weak. He can't
get started on anything unless he's pushed.

GORDON

[*Moving a little nearer—searching her face—thinking*]
She doesn't seem to like him so much . . . but I saw her
kiss him! . . .

EVANS

[*Surprised*]
Oh, come now, Nina, aren't you being a little hard on Ned?
It's true he's sort of lost his grip in a way but he's our best
friend.

GORDON

[*Moving away from his father again—resentfully—thinking*]

What's Dad standing up for him to her for? . . .

NINA

[*Thinking triumphantly*]

That's right, Sam . . . just what I wanted you to say!
. . .

[*Boredly*]

Oh, I know he is but he gets on my nerves hanging around all
the time. Without being too rude, I urged him to get back
to his work, and made him promise me he wouldn't return
for two years. Finally he promised—and then he became
silly and sentimental and asked me to kiss him good-bye for
good luck! So I kissed him to get rid of him! The silly
fool!

GORDON

[*Thinking—overjoyed*]

Then! . . . that's why! . . . that's why! . . . and he'll
be gone two years! . . . oh, I'm so glad! . . .

[*He goes to her and looks up into her face with shining
eyes*]

Mother!

NINA

Dear!

[*She takes him up on her lap and hugs him in her arms*]

GORDON

[*Kisses her*]

There!

[*Triumphantly thinking*]

That makes up for his kiss! . . . That takes it off her mouth. . . .

EVANS

[*Grinning*]

Ned must be falling for you—in his old age!

[*Then sentimentally*]

Poor guy! He's never married, that's the trouble. He's lonely. I know how he feels. A fellow needs a little feminine encouragement to help him keep his head up.

NINA

[*Snuggling* GORDON's *head against hers—laughing teasingly*]

I think your hard-headed Dad is getting mushy and silly! What do you think, Gordon?

GORDON

[*Laughing with her*]

Yes, he's mushy, Mother! He's silly!

[*He kisses her and whispers*]

I'm going to be like Gordon Shaw, Mother!

[*She hugs him fiercely to her, triumphantly happy*]

EVANS

[*Grinning*]

You two are getting too hard-boiled for me.

[*He laughs. They all laugh happily together*]

NINA

[*Suddenly overcome by a wave of conscience-stricken remorse and pity*]

Oh, I am hard on Ned! . . . poor dear generous Ned!

. . . you told me to lie to your son against you . . .
for my sake . . . I'm not worthy of your love! . . . I'm
low and selfish! . . . but I do love you! . . . this is the
son of our love in my arms! . . . oh, Mother God, grant
my prayer that some day we may tell our son the truth
and he may love his father! . . .

GORDON

[*Sensing her thoughts, sits up in her lap and stares into
her face, while she guiltily avoids his eyes—in fear and
resentment*]
[*Thinking*]
She's thinking about that Darrell now! . . . I know!
. . . she likes him too! . . . she can't fool me! . . . I
saw her kissing! . . . she didn't think he was a silly fool
then! . . . she was lying to Dad and me! . . .
[*He pushes off her lap and backs away from her*]

NINA

[*Thinking frightenedly*]
He read my thoughts! . . . I mustn't even think of Ned
when he's around! . . . poor Ned! . . . no, don't think
of him! . . .
[*Leaning forward toward* GORDON *with her arms stretched
out entreatingly but adopting a playful tone*]
Why, Gordon, what's come over you? You jumped off my
lap as though you'd sat on a tack!
[*She forces a laugh*]

GORDON

[*His eyes on the floor—evasively*]
I'm hungry. I want to see if lunch is nearly ready.
[*He turns abruptly and runs out*]

EVANS

[*In a tone of superior manly understanding, kindly but laying down the law to womanly weakness*]

He's sick of being babied, Nina. You forget he's getting to be a big boy. And we want him to grow up a real he-man and not an old lady like Charlie.

[*Sagaciously*]

That's what's made Charlie like he is, I'll bet. His mother never stopped babying him.

NINA

[*Submissively—but with a look of bitter scorn at him*]

Perhaps you're right, Sam.

EVANS

[*Confidently*]

I know I am!

NINA

[*Thinking with a look of intense hatred*]

Oh, Mother God, grant that I may some day tell this fool the truth! . . .

CURTAIN

ACT EIGHT

ACT EIGHT

SCENE: *Late afternoon in late June, ten years later—the
afterdeck of the* EVANS' *motor cruiser anchored in the
lane of yachts near the finish line at Poughkeepsie. The
bow and amidship of the cruiser are off right, pointed
upstream. The portside rail is in the rear, the curve of
the stern at left, the rear of the cabin with broad windows and a door is at right. Two wicker chairs are at
left and a chaise longue at right. A wicker table with
another chair is at center. The afterdeck is in cool
shade, contrasted with the soft golden haze of late
afternoon sunlight that glows on the river.*

NINA *is sitting by the table at center,* DARRELL *in the
chair farthest left,* MARSDEN *in the chaise longue at
right.* EVANS *is leaning over the rail directly back
of* NINA, *looking up the river through a pair of
binoculars.* MADELINE ARNOLD *is standing by his
side.*

NINA'S *hair has turned completely white. She is desperately trying to conceal the obvious inroads of time
by an over-emphasis on make-up that defeats its end by
drawing attention to what it would conceal. Her face
is thin, her cheeks taut, her mouth drawn with forced
smiling. There is little left of her face's charm except
her eyes which now seem larger and more deeply mysterious than ever. But she has kept her beautiful figure.*

277

It has the tragic effect of making her face seem older and more worn-out by contrast. Her general manner recalls instantly the NINA *of Act Four, neurotic, passionately embittered and torn. She is dressed in a white yachting costume.*

DARRELL *seems to have "thrown back" to the young doctor we had seen at the house of* NINA's *father in Act Two. He has again the air of the cool, detached scientist regarding himself and the people around him as interesting phenomena. In appearance, he is once more sharply defined, his face and body have grown lean and well-conditioned, the puffiness and jowls of the previous Act are gone. His skin is tanned almost black by his years in the tropics. His thick hair is iron-gray. He wears flannel pants, a blue coat, white buckskin shoes. He looks his fifty-one years, perhaps, but not a day more.*

MARSDEN *has aged greatly. The stoop of his tall figure is accentuated, his hair has grown whitish. He is an older image of the* MARSDEN *of Act Five, who was so prostrated by his mother's death. Now it is his sister's death two months before that has plunged him into despair. His present grief, however, is more resigned to its fate than the old. He is dressed immaculately in black, as in Act Five.*

EVANS *is simply* EVANS, *his type logically developed by ten years of continued success and accumulating wealth, jovial and simple and good-natured as ever, but increasingly stubborn and self-opinionated. He has grown very stout. His jowly broad face has a heavy, flushed, apoplectic look. His head has grown quite bald on top.*

*He is wearing a yachting cap, blue yachting coat, white
flannel pants, buckskin shoes.*

MADELINE ARNOLD *is a pretty girl of nineteen, with dark
hair and eyes.   Her skin is deeply tanned, her figure tall
and athletic, reminding one of* NINA's *when we first saw
her. Her personality is direct and frank. She gives the
impression of a person who always knows exactly what
she is after and generally gets it, but is also generous
and a good loser, a good sport who is popular with her
own sex as well as sought after by men. She is dressed
in a bright-colored sport costume.*

EVANS

[*Nervous and excited—on pins and needles—lowering his
binoculars impatiently*]

Can't see anything up there!   There's a damned haze on the
river!

[*Handing the binoculars to* MADELINE]

Here, Madeline.   You've got young eyes.

MADELINE

[*Eagerly*]

Thank you.

[*She looks up the river through the glasses*]

NINA

[*Thinking—bitterly*]

Young eyes! . . . they look into Gordon's eyes! . . . he
sees love in her young eyes! . . . mine are old now! . . .

EVANS

[*Pulling out his watch*]

Soon be time for the start.

[*Comes forward—exasperatedly*]

Of course, the damned radio has to pick out this time to go dead! Brand new one I had installed especially for this race, too! Just my luck!

[*Coming to* NINA *and putting his hand on her shoulder*]

Gosh, I'll bet Gordon's some keyed-up right at this moment, Nina!

MADELINE

[*Without lowering the glasses*]

Poor kid! I'll bet he is!

NINA

[*Thinking with intense bitterness*]

That tone in her voice! . . . her love already possesses him! . . . my son! . . .

[*Vindictively*]

But she won't! . . . as long as I live! . . .

[*Flatly*]

Yes, he must be nervous.

EVANS

[*Taking his hand away, sharply*]

I didn't mean nervous. He doesn't know what it is to have nerves. Nothing's ever got him rattled yet.

[*This last with a resentful look down at her as he moves back to the rail*]

MADELINE

[*With the calm confidence of one who knows*]

Yes, you can bank on Gordon never losing his nerve.

NINA

[*Coldly*]

I'm quite aware my son isn't a weakling—

[*Meaningly, with a glance at* MADELINE]
even though he does do weak things sometimes.

MADELINE

[*Without lowering the glasses from her eyes—thinking good-naturedly*]
Ouch! . . . that was meant for me! . . .
[*Then hurt*]
Why does she dislike me so? . . . I've done my best, for Gordon's sake, to be nice to her. . . .

EVANS

[*Looking back at* NINA *resentfully—thinking*]
Another nasty crack at Madeline! . . . Nina's certainly become the prize bum sport! . . . I thought once her change of life was over she'd be ashamed of her crazy jealousy . . . instead of that it's got worse . . . but I'm not going to let her come between Gordon and Madeline . . . he loves her and she loves him . . . and her folks have got money and position, too . . . and I like her a lot . . . and, by God, I'm going to see to it their marriage goes through on schedule, no matter how much Nina kicks up! . . .

DARRELL

[*Keenly observant—thinking*]
Nina hates this young lady . . . of course! . . . Gordon's girl . . . she'll smash their engagement if she can . . . as she did mine once . . . once! . . . thank God my slavery is over! . . . how did she know I was back in town? . . . I wasn't going to see her again . . . but her invitation was so imploring . . . my duty to Gordon, she wrote . . . what duty? . . . pretty late in the day! . . . that's better left dead, too! . . .

EVANS

[*Looking at his watch again*]

They ought to be lined up at the start any minute now.

[*Pounding his fist on the rail—letting his pent-up feelings explode*]

Come on, Gordon!

NINA

[*Startled—with nervous irritation*]

Sam! I told you I have a splitting headache!

[*Thinking intensely*]

You vulgar boor! . . . Gordon's engagement to her is all your fault! . . .

EVANS

[*Resentfully*]

I'm sorry. Why don't you take some aspirin?

[*Thinking irritably*]

Nina in the dumps! . . . Charlie in mourning! . . . what a pair of killjoys! . . . I wanted to bring Gordon and his friends on board to celebrate . . . no chance! . . . have to take Madeline . . . stage a party in New York . . . leave this outfit flat . . . Nina'll be sore as the devil but she'll have to like it . . .

DARRELL

[*Examining* NINA *critically—thinking*]

She's gotten into a fine neurotic state . . . reminds me of when I first knew her . . .

[*Then exultantly*]

Thank God, I can watch her objectively again . . . these last three years away have finally done it . . . complete cure! . . .

[*Then remorsefully*]
Poor Nina! . . . we're all deserting her . . .
[*Then glancing at* MARSDEN—*with a trace of a sneer*]
Even Marsden seems to have left her for the dead! . . .

MARSDEN

[*Vaguely irritated—thinking*]
What am I doing here? . . . what do I care about this
stupid race?. . . . why did I let Nina bully me into coming? . . . I ought to be alone . . . with my memories
of dear Jane . . . it will be two months ago Saturday she
died . . .
[*His lips tremble, tears come to his eyes*]

MADELINE

[*With an impatient sigh, lowering the glasses*]
It's no use, Mr. Evans, I can't see a thing.

EVANS

[*With angry disgust*]
If only that damned radio was working!

NINA

[*Exasperatedly*]
For heaven's sake, stop swearing so much!

EVANS

[*Hurt—indignantly*]
What about it if I am excited? Seems to me you could show
a little more interest without it hurting you, when it's Gordon's last race, his last appearance on a varsity!
[*He turns away from her*]

MADELINE

[*Thinking*]

He's right . . . she's acting rotten . . . if I were Gordon's mother, I certainly wouldn't . . .

EVANS

[*Turning back to* NINA—*resentfully*]

You used to cheer loud enough for Gordon Shaw! And our Gordon's got him beat a mile, as an oarsman, at least!

[*Turning to* DARRELL]

And that isn't father stuff either, Ned! All the experts say so!

DARRELL

[*Cynically*]

Oh, come on, Sam! Surely no one could ever touch Shaw in anything!

[*He glances at* NINA *with a sneer*]

[*Immediately angry at himself*]

What an idiot! . . . that popped out of me! . . . old habit! . . . I haven't loved her in years! . . .

NINA

[*Thinking indifferently*]

Ned still feels jealous . . . that no longer pleases me . . . I don't feel anything . . . except that I must get him to help me. .

[*She turns to* DARRELL *bitterly*]

Sam said "our" Gordon. He means his. Gordon's become so like Sam, Ned, you won't recognize him!

MADELINE

[*Thinking indignantly*]

She's crazy! . . . he's nothing like his father! . . . he's so strong and handsome! . . .

EVANS

[*Good-naturedly, with a trace of pride*]

You flatter me, Nina. I wish I thought that. But he isn't a bit like me, luckily for him. He's a dead ringer for Gordon Shaw at his best.

MADELINE

[*Thinking*]

Shaw . . . I've seen his picture in the gym . . . my Gordon is better looking . . . he once told me Shaw was an old beau of his mother's . . . they say she was beautiful once . . .

NINA

[*Shaking her head—scornfully*]

Don't be modest, Sam. Gordon *is* you. He may be a fine athlete like Gordon Shaw, because you've held that out to him as your ideal, but there the resemblance ceases. He isn't really like him at all, not the slightest bit!

EVANS

[*Restraining his anger with difficulty—thinking*]

I'm getting sick of this! . . . she's carrying her jealous grouch too far! . . .

[*Suddenly exploding, pounds his fist on the rail*]

Damn it, Nina, if you had any feeling you couldn't—right at the moment when he's probably getting into the shell—

[*He stops, trying to control himself, panting, his face red*]

NINA

[*Staring at him with repulsion—with cool disdain*]

I didn't say anything so dire, did I—merely that Gordon resembles you in character.

[*With malice*]

Don't get so excited.   It's bad for your high blood pressure.
Ask Ned if it isn't.

[*Intensely—thinking*]
If he'd only die! . . .
[*Thinking—immediately*]
Oh, I don't mean that . . . I mustn't . . .

DARRELL

[*Thinking keenly*]
There's a death wish . . . things have gone pretty far
. . . Sam does look as if he might have a bad pres-
sure . . . what hope that would have given me at one
time! . . . no more, thank God! . . .
[*In a joking tone*]

Oh, I guess Sam's all right, Nina.

EVANS

[*Gruffly*]

I never felt better.

[*He jerks out his watch again*]

Time for the start.   Come on in the cabin, Ned, and shoot a
drink.   We'll see if McCabe's getting the damned radio fixed.

[*Passing by* MARSDEN *he claps him on the shoulder exasperatedly*]

Come on, Charlie!   Snap out of it!

MARSDEN

[*Startled out of his trance—bewilderedly*]
Eh?—what is it?—are they coming?

EVANS

[*Recovering his good nature—with a grin, taking his
arm*]

You're coming to shoot a drink.   You need about ten, I think, to get you in the right spirit to see the finish!

[*To* Darrell *who has gotten up but is still standing by his chair*]

Come on, Ned.

NINA

[*Quickly*]

No, leave Ned with me.   I want to talk to him.   Take Madeline—and Charlie.

MARSDEN

[*Looking at her appealingly*]

But I'm perfectly contented sitting—

[*Then after a look in her eyes—thinking*]

She wants to be alone with Darrell . . . all right . . . doesn't matter now . . . their love is dead . . . but there's still some secret between them she's never told me . . . never mind . . . she'll tell me sometime . . . I'm all she will have left . . . soon. . . .

[*Then stricken with guilt*]

Poor dear Jane! . . . how can I think of anyone but you! . . . God, I'm contemptible! . . . I'll get drunk with that fool! . . . that's all I'm good for! . . .

MADELINE

[*Thinking resentfully*]

She takes a fine do-this-little-girl tone toward me! . . . I'll give in to her now . . . but once I'm married! . . .

EVANS

Come on then, Madeline.   We'll give you a small one.

[*Impatiently*]

Charlie!   Head up!

MARSDEN

[*With hectic joviality*]
I hope it's strong poison!

EVANS

[*Laughing*]
That's the spirit! We'll make a sport out of you yet!

MADELINE

[*Laughing, goes and takes* MARSDEN's *arm*]
I'll see you get home safe, Mr. Marsden!

[*They go into the cabin,* EVANS *following them.* NINA *and* DARRELL *turn and look at each other wonderingly, inquisitively, for a long moment.* DARRELL *remains standing and seems to be a little uneasy*]

DARRELL

[*Thinking with melancholy interest*]
And now? . . . what? . . . I can look into her eyes . . .
strange eyes that will never grow old . . . without desire or jealousy or bitterness . . . was she ever my mistress? . . . can she be the mother of my child? . . .
is there such a person as my son? . . . I can't think of these things as real any more . . . they must have happened in another life. . . .

NINA

[*Thinking sadly*]
My old lover . . . how well and young he looks . . . now we no longer love each other at all . . . our account with God the Father is settled . . . afternoons of happiness paid for with years of pain . . . love, passion, ecstasy . . . in what a far-off life were they alive! . . . the only living life is in the past and future . . . the present is an

interlude . . . strange interlude in which we call on past
and future to bear witness we are living! . . .

[*With a sad smile*]

Sit down, Ned. When I heard you were back I wrote you
because I need a friend. It has been so long since we loved
each other we can now be friends again. Don't you feel that?

DARRELL

[*Gratefully*]

Yes. I do.

[*He sits down in one of the chairs at left, drawing it up
closer to her*]

[*Thinking cautiously*]

I want to be her friend . . . but I will never . . .

NINA

[*Thinking cautiously*]

I must keep very cool and sensible or he won't help
me. . . .

[*With a friendly smile*]

I haven't seen you look so young and handsome since I first
knew you. Tell me your secret.

[*Bitterly*]

I need it! I'm old! Look at me! And I was actually looking forward to being old! I thought it would mean peace.
I've been sadly disillusioned!

[*Then forcing a smile*]

So tell me what fountain of youth you've found.

DARRELL

[*Proudly*]

That's easy. Work! I've become as interested in biology as
I once was in medicine. And not selfishly interested, that's

the difference. There's no chance of my becoming a famous biologist and I know it. I'm very much a worker in the ranks. But our Station is a "huge success," as Sam would say. We've made some damned important discoveries. I say "we." I really mean Preston. You may remember I used to write you about him with enthusiasm. He's justified it. He *is* making his name world-famous. He's what I might have been—I did have the brains, Nina!—if I'd had more guts and less vanity, if I'd hewn to the line!

[*Then forcing a smile*]

But I'm not lamenting. I've found myself in helping him. In that way I feel I've paid my debt—that his work is partly my work. And he acknowledges it. He possesses the rare virtue of gratitude.

[*With proud affection*]

He's a fine boy, Nina! I suppose I should say man now he's in his thirties.

NINA

[*Thinking with bitter sorrow*]

So, Ned . . . you remember our love . . . with bitterness! . . . as a stupid mistake! . . . the proof of a gutless vanity that ruined your career! . . . oh! . . .

[*Then controlling herself—thinking cynically*]

Well, after all, how do I remember our love? . . . with no emotion at all, not even bitterness! . . .

[*Then with sudden alarm*]

He's forgotten Gordon for this Preston! . . .

[*Thinking desperately*]

I must make him remember Gordon is his child or I can never persuade him to help me! . . .

[*Reproachfully*]

So you have found a son while I was losing mine—who is
yours, too!

DARRELL

[*Struck by this—impersonally interested*]
That's never occurred to me but now I think of it—
      [*Smiling*]
Yes, perhaps unconsciously Preston is a compensating substitute. Well, it's done both of us good and hasn't harmed
anyone.

NINA

[*With bitter emphasis*]
Except your real son—and me—but we don't count, I
suppose!

DARRELL

[*Coolly*]
Harmed Gordon? How? He's all right, isn't he?
      [*With a sneer*]
I should say from all I've been hearing that he was your
ideal of college hero—like his never-to-be-forgotten namesake!

NINA

[*Thinking resentfully*]
He's sneering at his own son! . . .
[*Then trying to be calculating*]
But I mustn't get angry . . . I must make him help me.
. . .
[*Speaking with gentle reproach*]
And am I the ideal of a happy mother, Ned?

DARRELL

[*Immediately moved by pity and ashamed of himself*]
Forgive me, Nina. I haven't quite buried all my bitterness,
I'm afraid.

[*Gently*]
I'm sorry you're unhappy, Nina.

NINA

[*Thinking with satisfaction*]
He means that . . . he still does care a little . . . if
only it's enough to . . . !
[*Speaking sadly*]
I've lost my son, Ned! Sam has made him all his. And it
was done so gradually that, although I realized what was
happening, there was never any way I could interfere. What
Sam advised seemed always the best thing for Gordon's future. And it was always what Gordon himself wanted, to
escape from me to boarding school and then to college, to become Sam's athletic hero—

DARRELL

[*Impatiently*]
Oh, come now, Nina, you know you've always longed for him
to be like Gordon Shaw!

NINA

[*Bursting out in spite of herself—violently*]
He's not like Gordon! He's forgotten me for that—!
[*Trying to be more reasonable*]
What do I care whether he's an athlete or not? It's such
nonsense, all this fuss! I'm not the slightest bit interested in

this race today, for example! I wouldn't care if he came in
last!

> [*Stopping herself—thinking frightenedly*]
> Oh, if he should ever guess I said that! . . .

DARRELL

> [*Thinking keenly*]
> Hello! . . . she said that as if she'd like to see him come
> last! . . . why? . . .
> [*Then vindictively*]
> Well, so would I! . . . it's time these Gordons took a
> good licking from life! . . .

MADELINE

> [*Suddenly appears in the door from the cabin, her face
> flushed with excitement*]

They're off! Mr. Evans is getting something—it's terribly
faint but—Navy and Washington are leading—Gordon's
third!

> [*She disappears back in the cabin*]

NINA

> [*Looking after her with hatred*]
> Her Gordon! . . . she is so sure! . . . how I've come to
> detest her pretty face! . . .

DARRELL

> [*Thinking with a sneer*]
> "Gordon's third"! . . . you might think there was no one
> else pulling the shell! . . . what idiots women make of
> themselves about these Gordons! . . . she's pretty, that
> Madeline! . . . she's got a figure like Nina's when I first
> loved her . . . those afternoons . . . age is beginning to

tell on Nina's face . . . but she's kept her wonderful body! . . .

[*With a trace of malice—dryly*]

There's a young lady who seems to care a lot whether Gordon comes in last or not!

NINA

[*Trying to be sorrowful and appealing*]

Yes. Gordon is hers now, Ned.

[*But she cannot bear this thought—vindictively*]

That is, they're engaged. But, of course, that doesn't necessarily mean— Can you imagine him throwing himself away on a little fool like that? I simply can't believe he really loves her! Why, she's hardly even pretty and she's deadly stupid. I thought he was only flirting with her—or merely indulging in a passing physical affair.

[*She winces*]

At his age, one has to expect—even a mother must face nature. But for Gordon to take her seriously, and propose marriage—it's too idiotic for words!

DARRELL

[*Thinking cynically*]

Oh, so you'll compromise on his sleeping with her . . . if you have to . . . but she must have no real claim to dispute your ownership, eh? . . . you'd like to make her the same sort of convenient slave for him that I was for you! . . .

[*Resentfully*]

I can't agree with you. I find her quite charming. It seems to me if I were in Gordon's shoes I'd do exactly what he has done.

[*In confusion—thinking bitterly*]
In Gordon's shoes! . . . I always was in Gordon Shaw's
shoes! . . . and why am I taking this young Gordon's
part? . . . what is he to me, for God's sake? . . .

NINA

[*Unheedingly*]
If he marries her, it means he'll forget me! He'll forget me
as completely as Sam forgot his mother! She'll keep him
away from me! Oh, I know what wives can do! She'll use
her body until she persuades him to forget me! My son,
Ned! And your son, too!
[*She suddenly gets up and goes to him and takes one of
his hands in both of hers*]
The son of our old love, Ned!

DARRELL

[*Thinking with a strange shudder of mingled attraction
and fear as she touches him*]
Our love . . . old love . . . old touch of her flesh . . .
we're old . . . it's silly and indecent . . . does she think
she still can own me? . . .

NINA

[*In the tone a mother takes in speaking to her husband
about their boy*]
You'll have to give Gordon a good talking to, Ned.

DARRELL

[*Still more disturbed—thinking*]
Old . . . but she's kept her wonderful body . . . how
many years since? . . . she has the same strange influence over me . . . touch of her flesh . . . it's danger-

ous . . . bosh, I'm only humoring her as a friend . . . as
her doctor . . . and why shouldn't I have a talk with
Gordon? . . . a father owes something to his son . . . he
ought to advise him. . . .
[*Then alarmed*]
But I was never going to meddle again . . .
[*Sternly*]
I swore I'd never again meddle with human lives, Nina!

NINA

[*Unheedingly*]
You must keep him from ruining his life.

DARRELL

[*Doggedly—struggling with himself*]
I won't touch a life that has more than one cell!
[*Harshly*]
And I wouldn't help you in this, anyway! You've got to give
up owning people, meddling in their lives as if you were God
and had created them!

NINA

[*Strangely forlorn*]
I don't know what you mean, Ned. Gordon is my son, isn't
he?

DARRELL

[*With a sudden strange violence*]
And mine! Mine, too!
[*He stops himself*]
[*Thinking*]
Shut up, you fool! . . . is that the way to humor
her? . . .

NINA

[*With strange quiet*]
I think I still love you a little, Ned.

DARRELL

[*In her tone*]
And I still love you a little, Nina.
[*Then sternly*]
But I will not meddle in your life again!
[*With a harsh laugh*]
And you've meddled enough with human love, old lady! Your
time for that is over! I'll send you a couple of million cells
you can torture without harming yourself!
[*Regaining control—shamefacedly*]
Nina! Please forgive me!

NINA

[*Starts as if out of a dream—anxiously*]
What were you saying, Ned?
[*She lets go of his hand and goes back to her chair*]

DARRELL

[*Dully*]
Nothing.

NINA

[*Strangely*]
We were talking about Sam, weren't we? How do you think
he looks?

DARRELL

[*Confusedly casual*]
Fine. A bit too fat, of course. He looks as though his

blood pressure might be higher than it ought to be. But
that's not unusual in persons of his build and age. It's nothing to hope——I meant, to worry over!

[*Then violently*]

God damn it, why did you make me say hope?

NINA

[*Calmly*]

It may have been in your mind, too, mayn't it?

DARRELL

No! I've nothing against Sam. I've always been his best
friend. He owes his happiness to me.

NINA

[*Strangely*]

There are so many curious reasons we dare not think about
for thinking things!

DARRELL

[*Rudely*]

Thinking doesn't matter a damn! Life is something in one
cell that doesn't need to think!

NINA

[*Strangely*]

I know! God the Mother!

DARRELL

[*Excitedly*]

And all the rest is gutless egotism! But to hell with it!
What I started to say was, what possible reason could I
have for hoping for Sam's death?

NINA

[*Strangely*]

We're always desiring death for ourselves or others, aren't we—while we while away our lives with the old surface ritual of coveting our neighbor's ass?

DARRELL

[*Frightenedly*]

You're talking like the old Nina now—when I first loved you. Please don't! It isn't decent—at our age!

[*Thinking in terror*]

The old Nina! . . . am I the old Ned? . . . then that means? . . . but we must not meddle in each other's lives again! . . .

NINA

[*Strangely*]

I am the old Nina! And this time I will not let my Gordon go from me forever!

EVANS

[*Appears in the doorway of the cabin—excited and irritated*]

Madeline's listening in now. It went dead on me.

[*Raising the binoculars as he goes to the rail, he looks up the river*]

Last I got, Gordon third, Navy and Washington leading. They're the ones to fear, he said—Navy especially.

[*Putting down the glasses—with a groan*]

Damned haze! My eyes are getting old.

[*Then suddenly with a grin*]

You ought to see Charlie! He started throwing Scotch into him as if he were drinking against time. I had to take the bottle away from him. It's hit him an awful wallop.

[*Then looking from one to the other—resentfully*]
What's the matter with you two? There's a race going on,
don't you know it? And you sit like dead clams!

DARRELL

[*Placatingly*]
I thought someone'd better stay out here and let you know
when they get in sight.

EVANS

[*Relieved*]
Oh, sure, that's right! Here, take the glasses. You always
had good eyes.

[DARRELL *gets up and takes the glasses and goes to the
rail and begins adjusting them*]

DARRELL

Which crew was it you said Gordon feared the most?

EVANS

[*Has gone back to the cabin doorway*]
Navy.

[*Then proudly*]
Oh, he'll beat them! But it'll be damn close. I'll see if
Madeline's getting—

[*He goes back in the cabin*]

DARRELL

[*Looking up the river—with vindictive bitterness—thinking*]
Come on, Navy! . . .

NINA

[*Thinking bitterly*]

Madeline's Gordon! . . . Sam's Gordon! . . . the thanks
I get for saving Sam at the sacrifice of my own happiness!
. . . I won't have it! . . . what do I care what happens
to Sam now? . . . I hate him! . . . I'll tell him Gordon
isn't his child! . . . and threaten to tell Gordon too,
unless! . . . he'll be in deadly fear of that! . . . he'll
soon find some excuse to break their engagement! . . . he
can! . . . he has the strangest influence over Gordon! . . .
but Ned must back me up or Sam won't believe me! . . .
Ned must tell him too! . . . but will Ned? . . . he'll be
afraid of the insanity! . . . I must make him believe
Sam's in no danger . . .

[*Intensely*]

Listen, Ned, I'm absolutely sure, from things she wrote me
before she died, that Sam's mother must have been deliberately lying to me about the insanity that time. She
was jealous because Sam loved me and she simply wanted to
be revenged, I'm sure.

DARRELL

[*Without lowering glasses—dryly*]

No. She told you the truth. I never mentioned it, but I
went up there once and made a thorough investigation of his
family.

NINA

[*With resentful disappointment*]

Oh—I suppose you wanted to make sure so you could hope
he'd go insane?

DARRELL

[*Simply*]

I needed to be able to hope that, then. I loved you horribly
at that time, Nina—horribly!

NINA

[*Putting her hands on his arm*]

And you don't—any more, Ned?

[*Thinking intensely*]

Oh, I must make him love me again . . . enough to make
him tell Sam! . . .

DARRELL

[*Thinking strangely—struggling with himself*]

She'd like to own me again . . . I wish she wouldn't
touch me . . . what is this tie of old happiness between
our flesh? . . .

[*Harshly—weakly struggling to shake off her hands,
without lowering the glasses*]

I won't meddle again with human lives, I told you!

NINA

[*Unheeding, clinging to him*]

And I loved you horribly! I still do love you, Ned! I used
to hope he'd go insane myself because I loved you so! But
look at Sam! He's sane as a pig! There's absolutely no
danger now!

DARRELL

[*Thinking—alarmed*]

What is she after now—what does she want me for? . . .

[*Stiffly*]

I'm no longer a doctor but I should say he's a healthy miss

of Nature's. It's a thousand to one against it at this late day.

NINA

[*With sudden fierce intensity*]

Then it's time to tell him the truth, isn't it? We've suffered all our lives for his sake! We've made him rich and happy! It's time he gave us back our son!

DARRELL

[*Thinking*]

Aha . . . so that's it! . . . tell Sam the truth? . . . at last! . . . by God, I'd like to tell him, at that! . . .

[*With a sneer*]

Our son? You mean yours, my dear! Kindly count me out of any further meddling with—

NINA

[*Unruffledly—obsessed*]

But Sam won't believe me if I'm the only one to tell him! He'll think I'm lying for spite, that it's only my crazy jealousy! He'll ask you! You've got to tell him too, Ned!

DARRELL

[*Thinking*]

I'd like to see his face when I told him this famous oarsman isn't his son but mine! . . . that might pay me back a little for all he's taken from me! . . .

[*Harshly*]

I've stopped meddling in Sam's life, I tell you!

NINA

[*Insistently*]

Think of what Sam has made us go through, of how he's

made us suffer! You've got to tell him! You still love me a
little, don't you, Ned? You must when you remember the
happiness we've known in each other's arms! You were
the only happiness I've ever known in life!

DARRELL

[*Struggling weakly—thinking*]
She lies! . . . there was her old lover, Gordon! . . . he
was always first! . . . then her son, Gordon! . . .
[*With desperate rancor—thinking*]
Come on, Navy! . . . beat her Gordons for me! . . .

NINA

[*Intensely*]
Oh, if I'd only gone away with you that time when you came
back from Europe! How happy we would have been, dear!
How our boy would have loved you—if it hadn't been for
Sam!

DARRELL

[*Thinking—weakly*]
Yes, if it hadn't been for Sam I would have been happy!
. . . I would have been the world's greatest neurologist!
. . . my boy would have loved me and I'd have loved
him! . . .

NINA

[*With a crowning intensity to break down his last re-
sistance*]
You must tell him, Ned! For my sake! Because I love you!
Because you remember our afternoons—our mad happiness!
Because you love me!

DARRELL

[*Beaten—dazedly*]

Yes—what must I do?—meddle again?

[*The noise of* MADELINE'S *excited voice cheering and clapping her hands, of* MARSDEN'S *voice yelling drunkenly, of* EVANS', *all shouting* "Gordon! Gordon! Come on, Gordon!" *comes from the cabin.* MARSDEN *appears swaying in the cabin doorway yelling* "Gordon!" *He is hectically tipsy.* DARRELL *gives a violent shudder as if he were coming out of a nightmare and pushes* NINA *away from him*]

DARRELL

[*Thinking—dazedly still, but in a tone of relief*]

Marsden again! . . . thank God! . . . he's saved me! . . . from her! . . . and her Gordons! . . .

[*Turning on her triumphantly*]

No, Nina—sorry—but I can't help you. I told you I'd never meddle again with human lives!

[*More and more confidently*]

Besides, I'm quite sure Gordon isn't my son, if the real deep core of the truth were known! I was only a body to you. Your first Gordon used to come back to life. I was never more to you than a substitute for your dead lover! Gordon is really Gordon's son! So you see I'd be telling Sam a lie if I boasted that I— And I'm a man of honor! I've proved that, at least!

[*He raises his glasses and looks up the river*]

[*Thinking exultantly*]

I'm free! . . . I've beaten her at last! . . . now come on, Navy! . . . you've got to beat her Gordons for me! . . .

NINA

[*After staring at him for a moment—walking away from him—thinking with a dull fatalism*]
I've lost him . . . he'll never tell Sam now . . . is what he said right? . . . is Gordon Gordon's? . . . oh, I hope so! . . . oh, dear, dead Gordon, help me to get back your son! . . . I must find some way. . . .
[*She sits down again*]

MARSDEN

[*Who has been staring at them with a foolish grin*]
Hello, you two! Why do you look so guilty? You don't love each other any more! It's all nonsense! I don't feel the slightest twinge of jealousy. That's proof enough, isn't it?
[*Then blandly apologetic*]
Pardon me if I sound a bit pipped—a good bit! Sam said ten and then took the bottle away when I'd had only five! But it's enough! I've forgotten sorrow! There's nothing in life worth grieving about, I assure you, Nina! And I've gotten interested in this race now.
[*He sings raucously*]
"Oh we'll row, row, row, right down the river! And we'll row, row, row—" Remember that old tune—when you were a little girl, Nina? Oh, I'm forgetting Sam said to tell you Gordon was on even terms with the leaders! A gallant spurt did it! Nip and tuck now! I don't care who wins— as long as it isn't Gordon! I don't like him since he's grown up! He thinks I'm an old woman!
[*Sings*]
"Row, row, row." The field against Gordon!

DARRELL

[*Hectically*]

Right!

[*He looks through the glasses—excitedly*]

I see a flashing in the water way up there! Must be their oars! They're coming! I'll tell Sam!

[*He hurries into the cabin*]

NINA

[*Thinking dully*]

He'll tell Sam . . . no, he doesn't mean that . . . I must find some other way . . .

MARSDEN

[*Walks a bit uncertainly to NINA's chair*]

Gordon really should get beaten today—for the good of his soul, Nina. That Madeline is pretty, isn't she? These Gordons are too infernally lucky—while we others—

[*He almost starts to blubber—angrily*]

we others have got to beat him today!

[*He slumps clumsily down to a sitting position on the deck by her chair and takes her hand and pats it*]

There, there, Nina Cara Nina! Don't worry your pretty head! It will all come out all right! We'll only have a little while longer to wait and then you and I'll be quietly married!

[*Thinking frightenedly*]

The devil! . . . what am I saying? . . . I'm drunk! . . . all right, all the better! . . . I've wanted all my life to tell her! . . .

Of course, I realize you've got a husband at present but, never mind, I can wait. I've waited a lifetime already; but

for a long while now I've had a keen psychic intuition that
I wasn't born to die before—

    [EVANS *and* MADELINE *and* DARRELL *come rushing out of
the cabin. They all have binoculars. They run to the
rail and train their glasses up the river*]

MADELINE

    [*Excitedly*]
I see them!
    [*Grabbing his arm and pointing*]
Look, Mr. Evans—there—don't you see?

EVANS

    [*Excitedly*]
No—not yet— Yes! Now I see them!
    [*Pounding on the rail*]
Come on, Gordon boy!

MADELINE

Come on, Gordon!
    [*The whistles and sirens from the yachts up the river
begin to be heard. This grows momentarily louder as
one after another other yachts join in the chorus as the
crews approach nearer and nearer until toward the close
of the scene there is a perfect pandemonium of sound*]

NINA

    [*With bitter hatred—thinking*]
How I hate her! . . .
    [*Then suddenly with a deadly calculation—thinking*]
Why not tell her? . . . as Sam's mother told me? . . .
of the insanity? . . . she thinks Gordon is Sam's son.
. . .

[*With a deadly smile of triumph*]
That will be poetic justice! . . . that will solve everything! . . . she won't marry him! . . . he will turn to me
for comfort! . . . but I must plan it out carefully! . . .

MARSDEN

[*Driven on—extravagantly*]
Listen, Nina! After we're married I'm going to write a
novel—my first real novel! All the twenty odd books I've
written have been long-winded fairy tales for grown-ups—
about dear old ladies and witty, cynical bachelors and quaint
characters with dialects, and married folk who always admire
and respect each other, and lovers who avoid love in hushed
whispers! That's what I've been, Nina—a hush-hush whis-
perer of lies! Now I'm going to give an honest healthy yell
—turn on the sun into the shadows of lies—shout "This is
life and this is sex, and here are passion and hatred and
regret and joy and pain and ecstasy, and these are men and
women and sons and daughters whose hearts are weak and
strong, whose blood is blood and not a soothing syrup!"
Oh, I can do it, Nina! I can write the truth! I've seen it
in you, your father, my mother, sister, Gordon, Sam, Darrell
and myself. I'll write the book of us! But here I am talking while my last chapters are in the making—right here
and now—

[*Hurriedly*]
You'll excuse me, won't you, Nina? I must watch—my duty
as an artist!

[*He scrambles to his feet and peers about him with a
hectic eagerness. NINA pays no attention to him*]

EVANS

[*Exasperatedly, taking down his glasses*]
You can't tell a damn thing—which is which or who's ahead
—I'm going to listen in again.

[*He hurries into the cabin*]

NINA

[*With a smile of cruel triumph—thinking*]
I can tell her . . . confidentially . . . I can pretend I'm
forced to tell her . . . as Sam's mother did with me
. . . because I feel it's due to her happiness and Gordon's . . . it will explain my objection to the engagement
. . . oh, it can't help succeeding . . . my Gordon will
come back! . . . I'll see he never gets away again! . . .

[*She calls*]
Madeline!

MARSDEN

[*Thinking*]
Why is she calling Madeline? . . . I must watch all
this carefully! . . .

EVANS

[*Comes rushing out in wild alarm*]
Bad news! Navy has drawn ahead—half a length—looks
like Navy's race, he said—

[*Then violently*]
But what does he know, that damn fool announcer—some
poor boob—!

MADELINE

[*Excitedly*]
He doesn't know Gordon! He's always best when he's pushed
to the limit!

NINA

[*She calls more sharply*]
Madeline!

DARRELL

[*Turns around to stare at her—thinking*]
Why is she calling Madeline? . . . she's bound she'll
meddle in their lives . . . I've got to watch her . . .
well, let's see. . . .
[*He touches* MADELINE *on the shoulder*]
Mrs. Evans is calling you, Miss Arnold.

MADELINE

[*Impatiently*]
Yes, Mrs. Evans. But they're getting closer. Why don't
you come and watch?

NINA

[*Not heeding—impressively*]
There's something I must tell you.

MADELINE

[*In hopeless irritation*]
But— Oh, all right.
[*She hurries over to her, glancing eagerly over her shoul-
der towards the river*]
Yes, Mrs. Evans?

DARRELL

[*Moves from the rail toward them—thinking keenly*]
I must watch this . . . she's in a desperate meddling
mood! . . .

NINA

[*Impressively*]

First, give me your word of honor that you'll never reveal a word of what I'm going to tell you to a living soul—above all not to Gordon!

MADELINE

[*Looking at her in amazement—soothingly*]

Couldn't you tell me later, Mrs. Evans—after the race?

NINA

[*Sternly—grabbing her by the wrist*]

No, now! Do you promise?

MADELINE

[*With helpless annoyance*]

Yes, Mrs. Evans.

NINA

[*Sternly*]

For the sake of your future happiness and my son's I've got to speak! Your engagement forces me to! You've probably wondered why I objected. It's because the marriage is impossible. You can't marry Gordon! I speak as your friend! You must break your engagement with him at once!

MADELINE

[*Cannot believe her ears—suddenly panic-stricken*]

But why—why?

DARRELL

[*Who has come closer—resentfully thinking*]

She wants to ruin my son's life as she ruined mine! . . .

NINA

[*Relentlessly*]

Why? Because—

DARRELL

[*Steps up suddenly beside them—sharply and sternly commanding*]

No, Nina!

[*He taps* MADELINE *on the shoulder and draws her aside.* NINA *lets go of her wrist and stares after them in a sort of stunned stupor*]

Miss Arnold, as a doctor I feel it my duty to tell you that Mrs. Evans isn't herself. Pay no attention to anything she may say to you. She's just passed through a crucial period in a woman's life and she's morbidly jealous of you and subject to queer delusions!

[*He smiles kindly at her*]

So get back to the race! And God bless you!

[*He grips her hand, strangely moved*]

MADELINE

[*Gratefully*]

Thank you. I understand, I think. Poor Mrs. Evans!

[*She hurries back to the rail, raising her glasses*]

NINA

[*Springing to her feet and finding her voice—with despairing accusation*]

Ned!

DARRELL

[*Steps quickly to her side*]

I'm sorry, Nina, but I warned you not to meddle.

[*Then affectionately*]

And Gordon is—well—sort of my stepson, isn't he?   I really want him to be happy.

[*Then smiling good-naturedly*]

All the same, I can't help hoping he'll be beaten in this race. As an oarsman he recalls his father, Gordon Shaw, to me.

[*He turns away and raises his glasses, going back to the rail.* NINA *slumps down in her chair again*]

EVANS

Damn! They all look even from here! Can you tell which is which, Madeline?

MADELINE

No—not yet—oh, dear, this is awful! Gordon!

NINA

[*Looking about her in the air—with a dazed question*]

Gordon?

MARSDEN

[*Thinking*]

Damn that Darrell! . . . if he hadn't interfered Nina would have told . . . something of infinite importance, I know! . . .

[*He comes and again sits on the deck by her chair and takes her hand*]

Because what, Nina—my dear little Nina Cara Nina—because what? Let me help you!

NINA

[*Staring before her as if she were in a trance—simply, like a young girl*]

Yes, Charlie. Yes, Father. Because all of Sam's father's
family have been insane. His mother told me that time so I
wouldn't have his baby. I was going to tell Madeline that
so she wouldn't marry Gordon. But it would have been a
lie because Gordon isn't really Sam's child at all, he's Ned's.
Ned gave him to me and I gave him to Sam so Sam could
have a healthy child and be well and happy. And Sam is
well and happy, don't you think?
[*Childishly*]
So I haven't been such an awfully wicked girl, have I,
Father?

MARSDEN

[*Horrified and completely sobered by what he has heard
—stares at her with stunned eyes*]
Nina! Good God! Do you know what you're saying?

MADELINE

[*Excitedly*]
There! The one on this side! I saw the color on their
blades just now!

EVANS

[*Anxiously*]
Are you sure? Then he's a little behind the other two!

DARRELL

[*Excitedly*]
The one in the middle seems to be ahead! Is that the Navy?
[*But the others pay no attention to him. All three are
leaning over the rail, their glasses glued to their eyes,
looking up the river. The noise from the whistles is now*

very loud. The cheering from the observation trains can be heard]

MARSDEN

[*Stares into her face with great pity now*]
Merciful God, Nina! Then you've lived all these years—
with this horror! And you and Darrell deliberately—?

NINA

[*Without looking at him—to the air*]
Sam's mother said I had a right to be happy too.

MARSDEN

And you didn't love Darrell then—?

NINA

[*As before*]
I did afterwards. I don't now. Ned is dead, too.
[*Softly*]
Only you are alive now, Father—and Gordon.

MARSDEN

[*Gets up and bends over her paternally, stroking her hair with a strange, wild, joyous pity*]
Oh, Nina—poor little Nina—my Nina—how you must have
suffered! I forgive you! I forgive you everything! I forgive even your trying to tell Madeline—you wanted to keep
Gordon—oh, I understand that—and I forgive you!

NINA

[*As before—affectionately and strangely*]
And I forgive you, Father. It was all your fault in the

beginning, wasn't it? You mustn't ever meddle with human lives again!

EVANS

[*Wildly excited*]
Gordon's sprinting, isn't he? He's drawing up on that middle one!

MADELINE

Yes! Oh, come on, Gordon!

DARRELL

[*Exultantly*]
Come on, Navy!

EVANS

[*Who is standing next to* NED, *whirls on him in a furious passion*]
What's that? What the hell's the matter with you?

DARRELL

[*Facing him—with a strange friendliness slaps him on the back*]
We've got to beat these Gordons, Sam! We've got to beat—

EVANS

[*Raging*]
You—!
[*He draws back his fist—then suddenly horrified at what he is doing but still angry, grabs* DARRELL *by both shoulders and shakes him*]
Wake up! What the hell's got into you? Have you gone crazy?

DARRELL

[*Mockingly*]
Probably! It runs in my family! All of my father's people were happy lunatics—not healthy, country folk like yours, Sam! Ha!

EVANS

[*Staring at him*]
Ned, old man, what's the trouble? You said "Navy."

DARRELL

[*Ironically—with a bitter hopeless laugh*]
Slip of the tongue! I meant Gordon! Meant **Gordon**, of course! Gordon is always meant—meant to win! Come on, Gordon! It's fate!

MADELINE

Here they come! They're both spurting! I can see **Gor-**don's back!

EVANS

[*Forgetting everything else, turns back to the race*]
Come on, boy! Come on, son!

[*The chorus of noise is now a bedlam as the crews near the finish line. The people have to yell and scream to make themselves heard*]

NINA

[*Getting up—thinking with a strange, strident, wild passion*]
I hear the Father laughing! . . . O Mother God, protect my son! . . . let Gordon fly to you in heaven! . . . quick, Gordon! . . . love is the Father's lightning! . . . Made-

line will bring you down in flames! . . . I hear His
screaming laughter! . . . fly back to me! . . .

[*She is looking desperately up into the sky as if some
race of life and death were happening there for her*]

EVANS

[*Holding on to a stanchion and leaning far out at the im-
minent risk of falling in*]

One spurt more will do it! Come on, boy, come on! It took
death to beat Gordon Shaw! You can't be beaten either,
Gordon! Lift her out of the water, son! Stroke! Stroke!
He's gaining! Now! Over the line, boy! Over with her!
Stroke! That's done it! He's won! He's won!

MADELINE

[*Has been shrieking at the same time*]

Gordon! Gordon! He's won! Oh, he's fainted! Poor dear
darling!

[*She remains standing on the rail, leaning out danger-
ously, holding on with one hand, looking down longingly
toward his shell*]

EVANS

[*Bounding back to the deck, his face congested and purple
with a frenzy of joy, dancing about*]

He's won! By God, it was close! Greatest race in the
history of rowing! He's the greatest oarsman God ever
made!

[*Embracing* NINA *and kissing her frantically*]

Aren't you happy, Nina? Our Gordon! The greatest ever!

NINA

[*Torturedly—trying incoherently to force out a last despairing protest*] .

No!—not yours!—mine!—and Gordon's!—Gordon is Gordon's!—he was my Gordon!—his Gordon is mine!

EVANS

[*Soothingly, humoring her—kissing her again*]
Of course he's yours, dear—and a dead ringer for Gordon Shaw, too! Gordon's body! Gordon's spirit! Your body and spirit, too, Nina! He's not like me, lucky for him! I'm a poor boob! I never could row worth a damn!

[*He suddenly staggers as if he were very drunk, leaning on* MARSDEN—*then gives a gasp and collapses inertly to the deck, lying on his back*]

MARSDEN

[*Stares down at him stupidly—then thinking strangely*]
I knew it! . . . I saw the end beginning! . . .
[*He touches* NINA's *arm—in a low voice*]
Nina—your husband!
[*Touching* DARRELL *who has stood staring straight before him with a bitter ironical smile on his lips*]
Ned—your friend! Doctor Darrell—a patient!

NINA

[*Stares down at* EVANS—*slowly, as if trying to bring her mind back to him*]
My husband?
[*Suddenly with a cry of pain, sinks on her knees beside the body*]
Sam!

DARRELL

[*Looking down at him—thinking yearningly*]
Is her husband dead . . . at last? . . .

[*Then with a shudder at his thoughts*]
No! . . . I don't hope! . . . I don't! . . .
[*He cries*]

Sam!

[*He kneels down, feels of his heart, pulse, looks into his face—with a change to a strictly professional manner*]

He's not dead. Only a bad stroke.

NINA

[*With a cry of grief*]
Oh, Ned, did all our old secret hopes do this at last?

DARRELL

[*Professionally, staring at her coldly*]
Bosh, Mrs. Evans! We're not in the Congo that we can believe in evil charms!
[*Sternly*]
In his condition, Mr. Evans must have absolute quiet and peace of mind or— And perfect care! You must tend him night and day! And I will! We've got to keep him happy!

NINA

[*Dully*]
Again?
[*Then sternly in her turn, as if swearing a pledge to herself*]
I will never leave his side! I will never tell him anything that might disturb his peace!

MARSDEN

[*Standing above them—thinking exultantly*]
I will not have long to wait now! . . .

[*Then ashamed*]
How can I think such things . . . poor Sam! . . . he
was . . . I mean he is my friend . . .
[*With assertive loyalty*]
A rare spirit! A pure and simple soul! A good man—
yes, a good man! God bless him!
[*He makes a motion over the body like a priest blessing*]

DARRELL

[*His voice suddenly breaking with a sincere human grief*]
Sam, old boy! I'm so damned sorry! I will give my life
to save you!

NINA

[*In dull anguish*]
Save—again?
[*Then lovingly, kissing* EVANS' *face*]
Dear husband, you have tried to make me happy, I will give
you my happiness again! I will give you Gordon to give
to Madeline!

MADELINE

[*Still standing on the rail, staring after* GORDON'S *shell*]
Gordon! . . . dear lover . . . how tired . . . but you'll
rest in my arms . . . your head will lie on my breast
. . . soon! . . .

CURTAIN

ACT NINE

ACT NINE

SCENE: *Several months later. A terrace on the* EVANS' *estate on Long Island. In the rear, the terrace overlooks a small harbor with the ocean beyond. On the right is a side entrance of the pretentious villa. On the left is a hedge with an arched gateway leading to a garden. The terrace is paved with rough stone. There is a stone bench at center, a recliner at right, a wicker table and armchair at left.*

It is late afternoon of a day in early fall. GORDON EVANS *is sitting on the stone bench, his chin propped on his hands,* MADELINE *standing behind him, her arm about his shoulders.* GORDON *is over six feet tall with the figure of a trained athlete. His sun-bronzed face is extremely handsome after the fashion of the magazine cover American collegian. It is a strong face but of a strength wholly material in quality. He has been too thoroughly trained to progress along a certain groove to success ever to question it or be dissatisfied with its rewards. At the same time, although entirely an unimaginative code-bound gentleman of his groove, he is boyish and likable, of an even, modest, sporting disposition. His expression is boyishly forlorn, but he is making a manly effort to conceal his grief.*

MADELINE *is much the same as in the previous Act except that there is now a distinct maternal older feeling*

325

in her attitude toward GORDON *as she endeavors to console him.*

MADELINE

[*Tenderly, smoothing his hair*]

There, dear! I know how horribly hard it is for you. I loved him, too. He was so wonderful and sweet to me.

GORDON

[*His voice trembling*]

I didn't really realize he was gone—until out at the cemetery—

[*His voice breaks*]

MADELINE

[*Kissing his hair*]

Darling! Please don't!

GORDON

[*Rebelliously*]

Damn it, I don't see why he had to die!

[*With a groan*]

It was that constant grind at the office! I ought to have insisted on his taking better care of himself. But I wasn't home enough, that's the trouble. I couldn't watch him.

[*Then bitterly*]

But I can't see why Mother didn't!

MADELINE

[*Reprovingly but showing she shares his feeling*]

Now! You mustn't start feeling bitter toward her.

GORDON

[*Contritely*]

I know I shouldn't.

[*But returning to his bitter tone*]

But I can't help remembering how unreasonably she's acted about our engagement.

MADELINE

Not since your father was taken sick, she hasn't, dear. She's been wonderfully nice.

GORDON

[*In the same tone*]

Nice? Indifferent, you mean! She doesn't seem to care a damn one way or the other any more!

MADELINE

You could hardly expect her to think of anyone but your father. She's been with him every minute. I never saw such devotion.

[*Thinking*]

Will Gordon ever get old and sick like that? . . . oh, I hope we'll both die before! . . . but I'd nurse him just as she did his father . . . I'll always love him! . . .

GORDON

[*Consoled—proudly*]

Yes, she sure was wonderful to him, all right!

[*Then coming back to his old tone*]

But—this may sound rotten of me—I always had a queer feeling she was doing it as a duty. And when he died, I

felt her grief was—not from love for him—at least, only
the love of a friend, not a wife's love.

[*As if under some urgent compulsion from within*]
I've never told you, but I've always felt, ever since I was a
little kid, that she didn't really love Dad. She liked him and
respected him. She was a wonderful wife. But I'm sure
she didn't love him.

[*Blurting it out as if he couldn't help it*]
I'll tell you, Madeline! I've always felt she cared a lot
for—Darrell.

[*Hastily*]
Of course, I might be wrong.

[*Then bursting out*]
No, I'm not wrong! I've felt it too strongly, ever since
I was a kid. And then when I was eleven—something hap-
pened. I've been sure of it since then.

MADELINE

[*Thinking in amazement, but not without a queer satisfaction*]
Does he mean that she was unfaithful to his father? . . .
no, he'd never believe that . . . but what else could he
mean? . . .

[*Wonderingly*]
Gordon! Do you mean you've been sure that your mother
was—

GORDON

[*Outraged by something in her tone—jumping to his feet
and flinging her hand off—roughly*]
Was what? What do you mean, Madeline?

MADELINE

[*Frightened—placatingly puts her arms around him*]
I didn't mean anything, dear. I simply thought you meant—

GORDON

[*Still indignant*]
All I meant was that she must have fallen in love with Darrell
long after she was married—and then she sent him away
for Dad's sake—and mine, too, I suppose. He kept coming
back every couple of years. He didn't have guts enough
to stay away for good! Oh, I suppose I'm unfair. I suppose it was damned hard on him. He fought it down, too,
on account of his friendship for Dad.
[*Then with a bitter laugh*]
I suppose they'll be getting married now! And I'll have to
wish them good luck. Dad would want me to. He was game.
[*With a bitter gloomy air*]
Life is damn queer, that's all I've got to say!

MADELINE

[*Thinking with a sort of tender, loving scorn for his
boyish naïveté*]
How little he knows her! . . . Mr. Evans was a fine man
but . . . Darrell must have been fascinating once . . . if
she loved anyone she isn't the kind who would hesitate
. . . any more than I have with Gordon . . . oh, I'll
never be unfaithful to Gordon . . . I'll love him always! . . .
[*She runs her fingers through his hair caressingly—
comfortingly*]

You must never blame them, dear. No one can help love. We couldn't, could we?

> [*She sits beside him. He takes her in his arms. They kiss each other with rising passion.* MARSDEN *comes in noiselessly from the garden, a bunch of roses and a pair of shears in his hands. He looks younger, calm and contented. He is dressed in his all black, meticulous, perfectly tailored mourning costume. He stands looking at the two lovers, a queer agitation coming into his face*]

MARSDEN

> [*Scandalized as an old maid—thinking*]

I must say! . . . his father hardly cold in his grave! . . . it's positively bestial! . . .

> [*Then struggling with himself—with a defensive self-mockery*]

Only it wasn't his father . . . what is Sam to Darrell's son? . . . and even if he were Sam's son, what have the living to do with the dead? . . . his duty is to love that life may keep on living . . and what has their loving to do with me? . . . my life is cool green shade wherein comes no scorching zenith sun of passion and possession to wither the heart with bitter poisons . . . my life gathers roses, coolly crimson, in sheltered gardens, on late afternoons in love with evening . . . roses heavy with after-blooming of the long day, desiring evening . . . my life is an evening . . . Nina is a rose, my rose, exhausted by the long, hot day, leaning wearily toward peace. . .

> [*He kisses one of the roses with a simple sentimental smile—then still smiling, makes a gesture toward the two lovers*]

That is on another planet, called the world . . . Nina and I have moved on to the moon. . . .

MADELINE

[*Passionately*]

Dear one! Sweetheart!

GORDON

Madeline! I love you!

MARSDEN

[*Looking at them—gaily mocking—thinking*]

Once I'd have felt jealous . . . cheated . . . swindled
by God out of joy! . . . I would have thought bitterly,
"The Gordons have all the luck!" . . . but now I know
that dear old Charlie . . . yes, poor dear old Charlie!—
passed beyond desire, has all the luck at last! . . .

[*Then matter-of-factly*]

But I'll have to interrupt their biological preparations
. . . there are many things still to be done this evening . . . Age's terms of peace, after the long interlude
of war with life, have still to be concluded . . . Youth
must keep decently away . . . so many old wounds may
have to be unbound, and old scars pointed to with pride,
to prove to ourselves we have been brave and noble!
. . .

[*He lets the shears drop to the ground. They jump
startledly and turn around. He smiles quietly*]

Sorry to disturb you. I've been picking some roses for
your mother, Gordon. Flowers really have the power to
soothe grief. I suppose it was that discovery that led to
their general use at funerals—and weddings!

[*He hands a rose to* MADELINE]

Here, Madeline, here's a rose for you. Hail, Love, we who
have died, salute you!

[*He smiles strangely. She takes the rose automatically,
staring at him uncomprehendingly*]

MADELINE

[*Thinking suspiciously*]
What a queer creature! . . . there's something uncanny!
. . . oh, don't be silly! . . . it's only poor old Charlie! . . .
[*She makes him a mocking curtsey*]
Thank you, Uncle Charlie!

GORDON

[*Thinking with sneering pity*]
Poor old guy! . . . he means well . . . Dad liked him.
. . .
[*Pretending an interest in the roses*]
They're pretty.
[*Then suddenly*]
Where's Mother—still in the house?

MARSDEN

She was trying to get rid of the last of the people. I'm
going in. Shall I tell her you want to see her? It would
give her an excuse to get away.

GORDON

Yes. Will you?
[MARSDEN *goes into the house on right*]

MADELINE

You'd better see your mother alone. I'll go down to the
plane and wait for you. You want to fly back before dark,
don't you?

GORDON

Yes, and we ought to get started soon.
[*Moodily*]

Maybe it would be better if you weren't here. There are some things I feel I ought to say to her—and Darrell. I've got to do what I know Dad would have wanted. I've got to be fair. He always was to everyone all his life.

MADELINE

You dear, you! You couldn't be unfair to anyone if you tried!

[*She kisses him*]

Don't be too long.

GORDON

[*Moodily*]

You bet I won't! It won't be so pleasant I'll want to drag it out!

MADELINE

Good-bye for a while then.

GORDON

So long.

[*He looks after her lovingly as she goes out right, rear, around the corner of the house*]

[*Thinking*]

Madeline's wonderful! . . . I don't deserve my luck . . . but, God, I sure do love her! . . .

[*He sits down on the bench again, his chin on his hands*]

It seems rotten and selfish to be happy . . . when Dad . . . oh, he understands, he'd want me to be . . . it's funny how I got to care more for Dad than for Mother . . . I suppose it was finding out she loved Darrell . . . I can remember that day seeing her kiss him . . . it did something to me I never got over . . . but she made Dad happy . . . she gave up her own happiness for his sake . . . that was certainly damn fine . . . that was

playing the game . . . I'm a hell of a one to criticize . . .
my own mother! . . .

[*Changing the subject of his thoughts abruptly*]
Forget it! . . . think of Madeline . . . we'll be married
. . . then two months' honeymoon in Europe . . . God,
that'll be great! . . . then back and dive into the business
. . . Dad relied on me to carry on where he left off . . .
I'll have to start at the bottom but I'll get to the top in a
hurry, I promise you that, Dad! . . .

[NINA *and* DARRELL *come out of the house on the right.
He hears the sound of the door and looks around*]
[*Thinking resentfully*]
Funny! . . . I can't stand it even now! . . . when I see
him with Mother! . . . I'd like to beat him up! . . .

[*He gets to his feet, his face unconsciously becoming
older and cold and severe. He stares accusingly at them
as they come slowly toward him in silence.* NINA *looks
much older than in the preceding Act. Resignation has
come into her face, a resignation that uses no make-up,
that has given up the struggle to be sexually attractive and
look younger. She is dressed in deep black.* DARRELL's
deep sunburn of the tropics has faded, leaving his skin a
Mongolian yellow. He, too, looks much older. His expression is sad and bitter*]

NINA

[*Glancing at* GORDON *searchingly—thinking sadly*]
He sent for me to say good-bye . . . really good-bye
forever this time . . . he's not my son now, nor Gordon's
son, nor Sam's, nor Ned's . . . he has become that
stranger, another woman's lover. . . .

DARRELL

[*Also after a quick keen glance at* GORDON's *face—thinking*]

There's something up . . . some final accounting . . .
[*Thinking resignedly*]
Well, let's get it over . . . then I can go back to work.
. . . I've stayed too long up here . . . Preston must be
wondering if I've deserted him. . . .
[*Then with a wondering sadness*]
Is that my son? . . . my flesh and blood? . . . staring at
me with such cold enmity? . . . how sad and idiotic this
all is! . . .

NINA

[*Putting on a tone of joking annoyance*]
Your message was a godsend, Gordon. Those stupid people
with their social condolences were killing me. Perhaps I'm
morbid but I always have the feeling that they're secretly
glad someone is dead—that it flatters their vanity and makes
them feel superior because they're living.
[*She sits wearily on the bench.* DARRELL *sits on side of
the recliner at right*]

GORDON

[*Repelled by this idea—stiffly*]
They were all good friends of Dad's. Why shouldn't they
be sincerely sorry? His death ought to be a loss to everyone who knew him.
[*His voice trembles. He turns away and walks to the
table*]
[*Thinking bitterly*]
She doesn't care a damn! . . . she's free to marry Darrell now! . . .

NINA

[*Thinking sadly, looking at his back*]
He's accusing me because I'm not weeping . . . well, I

did weep . . . all I could . . . there aren't many tears
left . . . it was too bad Sam had to die . . . living suited
him . . . he was so contented with himself . . . but I
can't feel guilty . . . I helped him to live . . . I made
him believe I loved him . . . his mind was perfectly
sane to the end . . . and just before he died, he smiled
at me . . . so gratefully and forgivingly, I thought . . .
closing our life together with that smile . . . that life is
dead . . . its regrets are dead . . . I am sad but there's
comfort in the thought that now I am free at last to rot
away in peace . . . I'll go and live in Father's old
home . . . Sam bought that back . . . I suppose he left
it to me . . . Charlie will come in every day to visit . . .
he'll comfort and amuse me . . . we can talk together of
the old days . . . when I was a girl . . . when I was
happy . . . before I fell in love with Gordon Shaw and
all this tangled mess of love and hate and pain and birth
began! . . .

DARRELL

[*Staring at* GORDON's *back resentfully*]
It gets under my skin to see him act so unfeelingly toward
his mother! . . . if he only knew what she's suffered for
his sake! . . . the Gordon Shaw ideal passed on through
Sam has certainly made my son an insensitive clod! . . .
[*With disgust*]
Bah, what has that young man to do with me? . . . compared to Preston he's only a well-muscled, handsome
fool! . . .
[*With a trace of anger*]
But I'd like to jolt his stupid self-complacency! . . . if
he knew the facts about himself, he wouldn't be sobbing
sentimentally about Sam . . . he'd better change his tune
or I'll certainly be tempted to tell him . . . there's no
reason for his not knowing now . . .

[*His face is flushed.   He has worked himself into a real anger*]

GORDON

[*Suddenly, having got back his control, turns to them— coldly*]
There are certain things connected with Dad's will I thought I ought to—
[*With a tinge of satisfied superiority*]
I don't believe Dad told you about his will, did he, Mother?

NINA

[*Indifferently*]
No.

GORDON

Well, the whole estate goes to you and me, of course.   I didn't mean that.
[*With a resentful look at* DARRELL]
But there is one provision that is peculiar, to say the least. It concerns you, Doctor Darrell—a half-million for your Station to be used in biological research work.

DARRELL

[*His face suddenly flushing with anger*]
What's that?   That's a joke, isn't it?
[*Thinking furiously*]
It's worse! . . . it's a deliberate insult! . . . a last sneer of ownership! . . . of my life! . . .

GORDON

[*Coldly sneering*]
I thought it must be a joke myself—but Dad insisted.

DARRELL

[*Angrily*]

Well, I won't accept it—and that's final!

GORDON

[*Coldly*]

It's not left to you but to the Station. Your supervision is mentioned but I suppose if you won't carry on, whoever is in real charge down there will be only too glad to accept it.

DARRELL

[*Stupefied*]

That means Preston! But Sam didn't even know Preston—except from hearing me talk about him! What had Sam to do with Preston? Preston is none of his business! I'll advise Preston to refuse it!

[*Thinking torturedly*]

But it's for science! . . . he has no right to refuse! . . . I have no right to ask him to! . . . God damn Sam! . . . wasn't it enough for him to own my wife, my son, in his lifetime? . . . now in death he reaches out to steal Preston! . . . to steal my work! . . .

NINA

[*Thinking bitterly*]

Even in death Sam makes people suffer . . .

[*Sympathetically*]

It isn't for you—nor for Preston. It's for science, Ned. You must look at it that way.

GORDON

[*Thinking resentfully*]

What a tender tone she takes toward him! . . . she's forgotten Dad already! . . .

[*With a sneer*]

You'd better accept. Half-millions aren't being thrown
away for nothing every day.

NINA

[*In anguish—thinking*]

How can Gordon insult poor Ned like that! . . . his own
father! . . . Ned has suffered too much! . . .

[*Sharply*]

I think you've said about enough, Gordon!

GORDON

[*Bitterly, but trying to control himself—meaningly*]

I haven't said all I'm going to say, Mother!

NINA

[*Thinking—at first frightenedly*]

What does he mean? . . . does he know about Ned being
. . . ?

[*Then with a sort of defiant relief*]

Well, what does it matter what he thinks of me? . . . he's
hers now, anyway. . . .

DARRELL

[*Thinking vindictively*]

I hope he knows the truth, for if he doesn't, by God, I'll
tell him! . . . if only to get something back from Sam of
all he's stolen from me! . . .

[*Authoritatively—as* GORDON *hesitates*]

Well, what have you got to say?   Your mother and I are
waiting.

GORDON

[*Furiously, taking a threatening step toward him*]
Shut up, you!   Don't take that tone with me or I'll forget
your age—
[*Contemptuously*]
and give you a spanking!

NINA

[*Thinking hysterically*]
Spanking! . . . the son spanks the father! . . .
[*Laughing hysterically*]
Oh, Gordon, don't make me laugh!   It's all so funny!

DARRELL

[*Jumps from his chair and goes to her—solicitously*]
Nina!   Don't mind him!   He doesn't realize—

GORDON

[*Maddened, comes closer*]
I realize a lot!   I realize you've acted like a cur!
[*He steps forward and slaps* DARRELL *across the face
viciously.* DARRELL *staggers back from the force of the
blow, his hands to his face.* NINA *screams and flings herself on* GORDON, *holding his arms*]

NINA

[*Piteously—hysterically*]
For God's sake, Gordon!   What would your father say?
You don't know what you're doing!   You're hitting your
father!

DARRELL

[*Suddenly breaking down—chokingly*]
No—it's all right, son—all right—you didn't know—

GORDON

[*Crushed, overcome by remorse for his blow*]
I'm sorry—sorry—you're right, Mother—Dad would feel
as if I'd hit him—just as bad as if I'd hit him!

DARRELL

It's nothing, son—nothing!

GORDON

[*Brokenly*]
That's damn fine, Darrell—damn fine and sporting of you!
It was a rotten, dirty trick! Accept my apology, Darrell,
won't you?

DARRELL

[*Staring at him stupidly—thinking*]
Darrell? . . . he calls me Darrell! . . . but doesn't he
know? . . . I thought she told him. . . .

NINA

[*Laughing hysterically—thinking*]
I told him he hit his father . . . but he can't understand
me! . . . why, of course he can't! . . . how could
he? . . .

GORDON

[*Insistently holding out his hand*]
I'm damned sorry! I didn't mean it! Shake hands, won't
you?

DARRELL

[*Doing so mechanically—stupidly*]

Only too glad—pleased to meet you—know you by reputa-
tion—the famous oarsman—great race you stroked last
June—but I was hoping the Navy would give you a beating.

NINA

[*Thinking in desperate hysterical anguish*]

Oh, I wish Ned would go away and stay away forever!
. . . I can't bear to watch him suffer any more! . . .
it's too frightful! . . . yes, God the Father, I hear you
laughing . . . you see the joke . . . I'm laughing too
. . . it's all so crazy, isn't it? . . .

[*Laughing hysterically*]

Oh, Ned! Poor Ned! You were born unlucky!

GORDON

[*Making her sit down again—soothing her*]

Mother! Stop laughing! Please! It's all right—all right
between us! I've apologized!

[*As she has grown calmer*]

And now I want to say what I was going to say. It wasn't
anything bad. It was just that I want you to know how
fine I think you've both acted. I've known ever since I was
a kid that you and Darrell were in love with each other.
I hated the idea on Father's account—that's only natural,
isn't it?—but I knew it was unfair, that people can't help
loving each other any more than Madeline and I could have
helped ourselves. And I saw how fair you both were to Dad
—what a good wife you were, Mother—what a true friend
you were, Darrell—and how damn much he loved you both!
So all I wanted to say is, now he's dead, I hope you'll get

married and I hope you'll be as happy as you both deserve—

> [*Here he breaks down, kissing her and then breaking away*]

I've got to say good-bye—got to fly back before dark—Madeline's waiting.

> [*He takes* DARRELL's *hand and shakes it again. They have both been staring at him stupidly*]

Good-bye, Darrell! Good luck!

DARRELL

> [*Thinking sufferingly*]
> Why does he keep on calling me Darrell . . . he's my boy . . . I'm his father . . . I've got to make him realize I'm his father! . . .
> [*Holding* GORDON's *hand*]

Listen, son. It's my turn. I've got to tell you something—

NINA

> [*Thinking torturedly*]
> Oh, he mustn't! . . . I feel he mustn't! . . .
> [*Sharply*]

Ned! First, let me ask Gordon a question.

> [*Then looking her son in the eyes, slowly and impressively*]

Do you think I was ever unfaithful to your father, Gordon?

GORDON

> [*Startled, stares at her—shocked and horrified—then suddenly he blurts out indignantly*]

Mother, what do you think I am—as rotten-minded as that!

> [*Pleadingly*]

Please, Mother, I'm not as bad as that! I know you're the best woman that ever lived—the best of all! I don't even except Madeline!

NINA

[With a sobbing triumphant cry]
My dear Gordon! You do love me, don't you?

GORDON

[Kneeling beside her and kissing her]
Of course!

NINA

[Pushing him away—tenderly]
And now go! Hurry! Madeline is waiting! Give her my love! Come to see me once in a while in the years to come! Good-bye, dear!
    [Turning to DARRELL, who is standing with a sad resigned expression—imploringly]
Did you still want to tell Gordon something, Ned?

DARRELL

[Forcing a tortured smile]
Not for anything in the world! Good-bye, son.

GORDON

Good-bye, sir.
    [He hurries off around the corner of the house at left, rear, thinking troubledly]
What does she think I am? . . . I've never thought that! . . . I couldn't! . . . my own mother! I'd kill myself if I ever even caught myself thinking . . . !
    [He is gone]

NINA

[*Turns to* NED, *gratefully taking his hand and pressing it*]
Poor dear Ned, you've always had to give! How can I ever thank you?

DARRELL

[*With an ironical smile—forcing a joking tone*]
By refusing me when I ask you to marry me! For I've got to ask you! Gordon expects it! And he'll be so pleased when he knows you turned me down.
[MARSDEN *comes out of the house*]
Hello, here comes Charlie. I must hurry. Will you marry me, Nina?

NINA

[*With a sad smile*]
No. Certainly not. Our ghosts would torture us to death!
[*Then forlornly*]
But I wish I did love you, Ned! Those were wonderful afternoons long ago! The Nina of those afternoons will always live in me, will always love her lover, Ned, the father of her baby!

DARRELL

[*Lifting her hand to his lips—tenderly*]
Thank you for that! And that Ned will always adore his beautiful Nina! Remember him! Forget me! I'm going back to work.
[*He laughs softly and sadly*]
I leave you to Charlie. You'd better marry him, Nina— if you want peace. And after all, I think you owe it to him for his life-long devotion.

MARSDEN

[*Thinking uneasily*]
They're talking about me . . . why doesn't he go? . . .
she doesn't love him any more . . . even now he's all
heat and energy and the tormenting drive of noon . . .
can't he see she is in love with evening? . . .
[*Clearing his throat uneasily*]
Do I hear my name taken in vain?

NINA

[*Looking at* MARSDEN *with a strange yearning*]
Peace! . . . yes . . . that is all I desire . . . I can no
longer imagine happiness . . . Charlie has found peace . . .
he will be tender . . . as my father was when I was a
girl . . . when I could imagine happiness . . .
[*With a girlish coquettishness and embarrassment—making way for him on the bench beside her—strangely*]
Ned's just proposed to me. I refused him, Charlie. I don't
love him any more.

MARSDEN

[*Sitting down beside her*]
I suspected as much. Then whom do you love, Nina Cara
Nina?

NINA

[*Sadly smiling*]
You, Charlie, I suppose. I have always loved your love
for me.
[*She kisses him—wistfully*]
Will you let me rot away in peace?

MARSDEN

[*Strongly*]

All my life I've waited to bring you peace.

NINA

[*Sadly teasing*]

If you've waited that long, Charlie, we'd better get married
tomorrow. But I forgot. You haven't asked me yet, have
you? Do you want me to marry you, Charlie?

MARSDEN

[*Humbly*]

Yes, Nina.

[*Thinking with a strange ecstasy*]

I knew the time would come at last when I would hear
her ask that! . . . I could never have said it, never! . . .
oh, russet-golden afternoon, you are a mellow fruit of
happiness ripely falling! . . .

DARRELL

[*Amused—with a sad smile*]

Bless you, my children!

[*He turns to go*]

NINA

I don't suppose we'll ever see you again, Ned.

DARRELL

I hope not, Nina. A scientist shouldn't believe in ghosts.

[*With a mocking smile*]

But perhaps we'll become part of cosmic positive and nega-
tive electric charges and meet again.

NINA

In our afternoons—again?

DARRELL

[*Smiling sadly*]
Again. In our afternoons.

MARSDEN

[*Coming out of his day dream*]
We'll be married in the afternoon, decidedly. I've already
picked out the church, Nina—a gray ivied chapel, full of
restful shadow, symbolical of the peace we have found. The
crimsons and purples in the windows will stain our faces
with faded passion. It must be in the hour before sunset
when the earth dreams in afterthoughts and mystic premoni-
tions of life's beauty. And then we'll go up to your old
home to live. Mine wouldn't be suitable for us. Mother
and Jane live there in memory. And I'll work in your
father's old study. He won't mind me.
[*From the bay below comes the roaring hum of an air-
plane motor. NINA and DARRELL jump startledly and
go to the rear of the terrace to watch the plane ascend
from the water, standing side by side. MARSDEN remains
oblivious*]

NINA

[*With anguish*]
Gordon! Good-bye, dear!
[*Pointing as the plane climbs higher moving away off
to the left—bitterly*]
See, Ned! He's leaving me without a backward look!

DARRELL

[*Joyfully*]

No! He's circling. He's coming back!

[*The roar of the engine grows steadily nearer now*]

He's going to pass directly over us!

[*Their eyes follow the plane as it comes swiftly nearer and passes directly over them*]

See! He's waving to us!

NINA

Oh, Gordon! My dear son!

[*She waves frantically*]

DARRELL

[*With a last tortured protest*]

Nina! Are you forgetting? He's my son, too!

[*He shouts up at the sky*]

You're my son, Gordon! You're my—

[*He controls himself abruptly—with a smile of cynical self-pity*]

He can't hear! Well, at least I've done my duty!

[*Then with a grim fatalism—with a final wave of his hand at the sky*]

Good-bye, Gordon's son!

NINA

[*With tortured exultance*]

Fly up to heaven, Gordon! Fly with your love to heaven! Fly always! Never crash to earth like my old Gordon! Be happy, dear! You've got to be happy!

DARRELL

[*Sardonically*]
I've heard that cry for happiness before, Nina! I remember
hearing myself cry it—once—it must have been long ago!
I'll get back to my cells—sensible unicellular life that floats
in the sea and has never learned the cry for happiness! I'm
going, Nina.
> [*As she remains oblivious, staring after the plane—
> thinking fatalistically*]
> She doesn't hear, either. . . .
> [*He laughs up at the sky*]
> Oh, God, so deaf and dumb and blind! . . . teach me to
> be resigned to be an atom! . . .
> [*He walks off, right, and enters the house*]

NINA

> [*Finally lowering her eyes—confusedly*]
Gone. My eyes are growing dim. Where is Ned? Gone,
too. And Sam is gone. They're all dead. Where are
Father and Charlie?
> [*With a shiver of fear she hurries over and sits on the
> bench beside* MARSDEN, *huddling against him*]
Gordon is dead, Father. I've just had a cable. What I
mean is, he flew away to another life—my son, Gordon,
Charlie. So we're alone again—just as we used to be.

MARSDEN

> [*Putting his arm around her—affectionately*]
Just as we used to be, dear Nina Cara Nina, before Gordon
came.

NINA

[*Looking up at the sky—strangely*]

My having a son was a failure, wasn't it? He couldn't give me happiness. Sons are always their fathers. They pass through the mother to become their father again. The Sons of the Father have all been failures! Failing they died for us, they flew away to other lives, they could not stay with us, they could not give us happiness!

MARSDEN

[*Paternally—in her father's tone*]

You had best forget the whole affair of your association with the Gordons. After all, dear Nina, there was something unreal in all that has happened since you first met Gordon Shaw, something extravagant and fantastic, the sort of thing that isn't done, really, in our afternoons. So let's you and me forget the whole distressing episode, regard it as an interlude, of trial and preparation, say, in which our souls have been scraped clean of impure flesh and made worthy to bleach in peace.

NINA

[*With a strange smile*]

Strange interlude! Yes, our lives are merely strange dark interludes in the electrical display of God the Father!

[*Resting her head on his shoulder*]

You're so restful, Charlie. I feel as if I were a girl again and you were my father and the Charlie of those days made into one. I wonder is our old garden the same? We'll pick flowers together in the aging afternoons of spring and summer, won't we? It will be a comfort to get home—to be old

and to be home again at last—to be in love with peace together—to love each other's peace—to sleep with peace
together—!
    [*She kisses him—then shuts her eyes with a deep sigh
    of requited weariness*]
—to die in peace! I'm so contentedly weary with life!

MARSDEN

    [*With a serene peace*]
Rest, dear Nina.
    [*Then tenderly*]
It has been a long day. Why don't you sleep now—as you
used to, remember?—for a little while?

NINA

    [*Murmurs with drowsy gratitude*]
Thank you, Father—have I been wicked?—you're so good—
dear old Charlie!

MARSDEN

    [*Reacting automatically and wincing with pain—thinking
    mechanically*]
God damn dear old . . . !
    [*Then with a glance down at NINA's face, with a happy
    smile*]
No, God bless dear old Charlie . . . who, passed beyond
desire, has all the luck at last! . . .
    [*NINA has fallen asleep. He watches with contented
    eyes the evening shadows closing in around them*]

CURTAIN